What's the Matter with the Church?

For my Harriman
Friends,
Bill Willis
December 10, 2005

What's the Matter with the Church?

A Call to Renewal

William Willis

Hope Publishing House
Pasadena, California

Library of Congress Cataloging-in-Publication Data

Willis, William, 1934-
    What's the matter with the church? : a call to renewal / William
Willis.-- 1st. ed.
        p. cm.
    ISBN 10: 1-932717-07-2 (pbk. : alk. paper)
    ISBN 13: 978-1-932717-07-5
    1. Church renewal. I. Title.
    BV600.3.W55 2005
    262'.001'7--dc22
                            2005016596

This book is dedicated to:

— *my wife Lynn, who has shared the experiences with the church that formed these ideas and convictions, who suggested it be written, and without whose constant encouragement and prodding it would never have been completed;*

— *to our children, James, Billy Lynn and Mary Belle, who walked the roads of joy and disappointment in the church with us (especially Billy Lynn who said he wanted to see his name in print!);*

— *and to Stephanie, who has come in recent years to share the spiritual journey with us.*

Contents

What's the Matter with the Church?

Acknowledgments

It is always impossible to acknowledge all of an author's sources and influences for what he has written, but it is most certainly the case for a work like this. My aim is to give an account of some things I have learned over an entire lifetime. My professors at Mercer University, Southeastern Baptist Theological Seminary and Harvard Divinity School provided me with a body of knowledge and widened my intellectual horizons, giving me a foundation on which my thought and experience developed.

My wife deserves the major credit for my undertaking this work. After hearing my ideas about the church for over 25 years, she insisted that I write about this and continued to "push" me to get it done, and then edited the manuscript several times along the way. I am grateful to Professor David Buttrick for his valuable suggestions for the manuscript, and to my friend and colleague Garth Duke-Barton for helping me "straighten out" the sequence and assisting me in countless instances with his computer expertise.

I was most fortunate to have Lee Gable, former academic dean of Lancaster Seminary, as a neighbor at Uplands Retirement Village when I was there on my sabbatical. His area of expertise is Christian Education, and at that very time I was at a loss as to how to approach that subject. What a gift it was for me to spend hours with him discussing the state of education in our churches. Unfortunately, he passed away before I could finish these essays.

Years ago I heard a quote from John Wesley about the importance of his small groups, the little societies. I spent hours searching for a reference to this effect but could not find it. When I asked Tom Albin, dean of the chapel at the Upper Room, about it, serendipitously he happened to have the reference at his finger-tips.

I have benefited immensely from scholars and preachers I have heard over the years, mostly at various meetings of the South Georgia Conference of the United Methodist Church. I am deeply indebted to the many speakers at these events, for they increased my store of knowledge and inspiration beyond measure.

I owe much gratitude to Faith Annette Sand of Hope Publishing House for her assistance in getting the manuscript ready for publication. She devoted much of her time to this project and I could not have gotten it done without her.

Foreword

William Willis is a wonder. We'll never pigeonhole him. He has marched with the leadership of the Civil Rights movement. He has led inner-city ministries in the North and preached to staunch parishes in the South below the Mason-Dixon line. He has bounced around among different denominations as if searching a place for God to place him. Wherever he is, he seems to gather around some of "God's Irregulars," those grand, if often secret, friends of Jesus who, like Bill himself, are free to follow unexpected byways of grace.

Now Bill Willis has written a book. In a series of brief essays he has probed the failings of American churches. He is critical, but in every chapter you sense he's a man gripped by the gospel message. He is a liberal but with a conservative confidence in the good wisdom of scripture. He is an Evangelical whose honesty will not let him tumble into "evangelicalist" cant. He clearly believes in the innovative energies of the Holy Spirit to shake us loose, turn us around and transform us "people of God" into a prophetic ministry. As you read, you will be dismayed by the church, but at the same time filled with dreams of possibility. Bill Willis is incurably ecumenical for he dreams a church united, holy, catholic and apostolic. And he believes that, in grace, churches can be useful servants of God.

We need Bill's candor. Mainline churches in our land are frightened, holding on to themselves for dear life; they are silent when they should speak and careless when they should care. They seem to have confused therapy with gospel and institutional management with mission. Of course, to be honest, these days it is difficult to be faithful in America. As a nation, we have cash and power, and both have corrupted us. Superpowers are seldom open to the presence of God. So how can God call forth faithful people in America? And how in the world will God reshape recalcitrant churches into prophetic preachers for our misguided land?

The book you hold is filled with insight, often unconsidered insight, that will stop you short and provoke thought. Bill Willis is a man driven by candor, but gripped by good hope. He knows he is called by God and that he wouldn't—couldn't—live outside of the church. So come meet William Willis and rethink your Christian self all over again.

—David Buttrick

DRUCILLA MOORE BUFFINGTON PROFESSOR OF HOMILETICS AND LITURGICS, EMERITUS, VANDERBILT UNIVERSITY DIVINITY SCHOOL

Preface

My faith journey has carried me over several theological terrains with each succeeding one enthusiastically rejecting the basic perspective of the former. When I was nine years old I sensed a calling to the Christian ministry that waned during my teenage years but reëmerged during my first year in college. I decided to enter the ministry and enrolled at Mercer University in Macon, Georgia, a Southern Baptist school. When I began my studies there I was a very staunch fundamentalist.

That stage did not last long. Before Christmas of that year my professors showed me the rationally untenable nature of that stance and I embarked on the theological exploration that has been the most rewarding and invigorating activity of my life. My theological interest continued in a liberal direction through my seminary and graduate school years, but I soon became frustrated with what I saw as the irrelevance of the church to life in that era, and in the late 1960s and early 70s I turned to political and social action to find more relevant involvement. This was the most exciting time in my life.

During those years I met and got to know a phenomenal number of political and social action leaders. I marched in Alabama and Mississippi with Dr. Martin Luther King, Jr., and my friendship with him has remained the richest treasure from that period in my life. I got to know Senator Robert Kennedy and served on his campaign committee. I have always felt the highest privilege of my life was serving as an honor guard for his casket at St. Patrick's Cathedral in New York City the night before his funeral. I have never felt such sadness as I did in 1968 when both of my heroes and friends were killed in the same year. But I am sure the most exciting experience in my life was riding in the limousine with Senator George McGovern to visit several of the state delegations at the 1968 Democratic Convention in Chicago.

In 1967, following the worst rioting in the history of our country, while serving as pastor of the First Congregational Church in Dearborn, Michigan, I was appointed by Governor George Romney to be chair of his statewide Fair Housing Committee. We got the fair housing bill passed in the Michigan legislature and helped get the federal fair housing bill passed in 1968. Although I had only a small part in getting this passed, I have never been prouder of any project I have worked on.

I also got to know Senator Edward Kennedy, Julian Bond, Senator Eugene McCarthy, Vice President Hubert Humphrey, Senator Walter Mondale, Shirley McLain, Sidney Portier, Pete Seeger and many others. It has always astounded me how many leaders I met in those years.

At the age of 44 I experienced a crisis of faith that brought me to a point of desperation and I made a decision to accept Jesus Christ as my Savior and Lord. My theology became wedded for the first time with a rich spiritual experience. In the years since then, the parallel roads of political and social concerns, personal Christian experience and intellectual interests have converged into a natural and comfortable theological direction. It definitely could not be considered conservative, but neither does the term liberal do justice because "liberal" means so many different things to people and because my position is also quite evangelical and even has some elements that are usually considered conservative.

Generally I believe it is the theological perspective that prevails at most mainline denominational seminaries and with those scholars whom mainline denominational professors respect. Although this term is not quite accurately descriptive, I have begun referring to it as a "common sense theology," because it encompasses common sense about the church's mission, about the Bible and about our work to establish the Kingdom of God on earth.

— *William Willis*, Harriman, Tennessee

What's the Matter with the Church?

Introduction

If the Shoe Fits

The opinions I bring to this discussion are intended as a critique of the Christian church, pointing out the main weaknesses and problems, as I see them, that need to be overcome if significant renewal of the church is to take place. I have no interest in "church bashing," but a genuine critique requires examining weaknesses as well as strengths. As a deeply grateful and enthusiastic supporter and admirer of the church, I could not discuss its shortcomings without citing its extraordinary accomplishments. So in each area of the church's life where I look at its problems I begin by crediting those things the church has done right in that area.

Even with the supreme regard I have for the church, when I listed all of its strengths, contributions and achievements I was amazed at how formidable these attributes are. It was actually a genuine epiphany for I had never fully grasped their volume or scope, nor thought how different the world would be without them. So I have not cited the benefits of the church – what it has done and still does for individuals and society – to make my criticisms of it more palatable, but because I could not do otherwise. These good, in many cases great, works are of such notable significance that not to mention them would be a glaring omission.

The direction and character of the renewal proposed by these chapters come from the perspective of one who is generally a liberal but who is willing to question traditional positions, even though some of the criticisms and suggestions might appear to belong to a conservative theological view. Sometimes mainline churches reject or ignore ideas and beliefs they should embrace because of their popularity in more conservative churches. Many in mainline churches need a clearer understanding of what their theology should be. As Bishop John Spong says of his Episcopal church, "We are not sure yet what we are, but we are sure we are not fundamentalists."

Obviously conservatism by definition is the opposite of renewal for it insists on maintaining the understandings, interpretations and values of the past, resisting any change. Since renewal of the church is clearly about change, the "old wine skins" of conservative thinking simply cannot hold the "new wine" of renewal. There is a basic need to overcome the legalism, idolatry and judgmentalism of conservatives, especially of fundamentalists, in order to bring new life and joyful commitment to the Body of Christ. Those who are staunchly dug in against renewal because they are self-righteously comfortable will obviously be left behind. Of course fundamentalism and conservatism will always appeal to many because there is safety in legalism when obeying a few strict rules puts them in the saintly sanctum.

In all probability the renewal I envision for the church will not result in an increase of its numbers. I believe it will produce a truer but far smaller Body of Christ. But it might result in as many or more additional members since there are many who have been turned off by the offensive baggage the church carries, so perhaps a renewed church might attract considerable growth among those who had been repelled but who would enjoy participating in the worship and fellowship of a renewed church. Approximately half of all Americans do not attend any church yet millions of them consider themselves "unchurched" Christians because they have wandered away from church attendance.

Fortunately there is not a single weakness of the church that has not been averted or overcome in congregations somewhere, past and present. I have encountered many wonderful churches through the years and a common denominator found in all these healthy and thriving churches is a substantial contingent of its members who are willing to undertake the task of correcting its mistakes. The title I chose for this book, *What's the Matter with the Church?* is actually a double entendre, for I didn't mean it only as "What's Wrong with the Church," but also as a reference to what are the important *matters* in the life and ministry of the church, and how they relate to one another in very profound ways.

I have come across an analogy between Noah's ark and the church several times that has always seemed quite apropos to me: The ark must have been a very unpleasant place with all those animals in such close quarters, and the ventilation couldn't have been that great! I'm sure the folks on board would have very much liked to go somewhere else, but their options were limited. Despite all that is wrong with the church, there is no viable alternative. In fact, my involvement in the Christian church, warts and all, has been the most rewarding and enriching experience of my life and it has made the crucial difference between a life of rich meaning and direction and one I feel would have been superficial and aimless by comparison.

A legitimate call to renewal must look at a panoply of problems often found in churches. I have served in five different denominations, read literature from many more, and have conversed on the subject with a wide range of clergy and laity. And now I have come upon pointers that I am confident could give us assistance on a road to renewal through very intentional and strategic efforts toward attitudinal changes. Obviously, mine is not a scholarly presentation about the church, but primarily a sharing of insights gained as an active participant over some 50 years.

Since any significant movement toward the solutions to most of the problems and errors of the church requires the mobilization of its laity, I especially want to appeal to lay people. One scholarly consideration, however, is pertinent. The discussion here falls into the traditional theological category called *dogmatics;* that refers to works addressed to the church, as opposed to *apologetics* which are addressed to the world outside the church. Arguing the merits of the church to those who do not subscribe to its main confessional values is beyond this project. As a confessing Christian I want to challenge the reader to become involved in a concerted effort to address the main weaknesses of the church.

I have always been a Methodist at heart and by family background, but I have also served Southern Baptist, United Church of Christ, Unitarian, and Presbyterian Church U.S.A. churches, and I have had the rewarding experience of preaching to congregations in almost all denominations, charismatic and Pentecostal, and even Catholic churches. I have been involved in many ecumenical efforts, and I have had close friendships with pastors in other communions wherever I have served and traveled.

It would appear that the people of God, wherever they find themselves, have a commonality of problems and failings. In fact, it has become evident that most of the church's shortcomings do not result from the nature of its organization, ministries or programs, or from the misguided views of its denominational or church leaders. Almost entirely they are the result of its members' attitudes. Thus, if by some absurdly unfeasible series of developments all Christian communions and congregations were brought under one ecclesiastical authority and one "ecumenical pope," probably nothing much would change. The church's members would still have the negative attitudes that are in need of renewal.

Our challenge is thus a call to lay people and clergy to join together with the Holy Spirit in an effort to accelerate the renewal of the church dramatically. This is the traditional task assigned to the Holy Spirit since the time Abraham was urged to follow the Lord's leading. But as it is with most problems that involve groups of people, there are no quick and easy answers which is presumably why we have not seen a major renewal in the church's life and ministry in decades. Too often we seek simplistic solutions. To be sure it is an awesome task. The population of the world is growing faster than the numbers of those we are reaching for Christ, but there are clear signs of a growing hunger in the world for the "Bread of Life." Truly the fields have never been "whiter for harvest" *(Jn 4:35)*.

As the Christian church is made up of human beings, it will never be without its faults. Yet those with vision as well as prophets and reformers in every age have never regarded human frailty as a reason for giving up. It has always been clear to them that inestimable growth and vitalization of the church are possible in spite of the errors and sins of its members and leaders. Therefore, these discussions of the imperfections and difficulties of the church are presented as the main bases for the attitudinal changes among church members that are critically needed for genuine church renewal to take place.

1

Seven Last Words

For when there is a change in the priesthood, there is necessarily a change in the law as well (Heb 7:12).

The Christian church has adapted its methods and approaches to an incredible variety of cultures, subcultures and local customs. It was commissioned to "go and make disciples of all nations" *(Mt 28:19),* so its basic mission has required a capability for adapting its ministries to a broad spectrum of cultural habits and needs around the world. Change has been an essential part of the fabric, the *matter,* of church history. Its message could never have reached so many people in the world if it had not been so capable of change.

Unfortunately, resisting change often hampers the ministry of Christian congregations around the world. It is a common characteristic of church life that it must contend with change every time significant proposals and in some cases even insignificant proposals are brought up for consideration. Someone has said the "seven last words of the church" are: "We have always done it this way."

We all resist change. This may be a normal human attitude, but that attitude must change so we can become people who are willing to be renewed. The Christian life requires us "to grow up in every way into him who is the head, into Christ" *(Eph 4:15),* in order to meet the standards set by Christ. Thus begins the conversion of our attitudes, feelings and behavior as we grow in christlikeness. These changes are proof positive the Holy Spirit is working in us to change us according to Christ's image. Resisting change is a serious *matter* for Christians for it has prevented many from accepting Jesus Christ as Lord, and has kept many of our church members at the lowest levels of "sanctification," frozen at the most elementary and immature levels of Christian attitudes and behavior.

We find outrageously unchristian attitudes even among long-time church members. Many consistently resist what is required of them by our faith. We find too often the church has been imprisoned by those who have no interest in being made into the likeness of Christ. Just think of the tremendous ministry that could happen in a church with a body of believers who are growing into closer relationships with the Lord with humbler, more caring attitudes.

Change is part of everyone's existence. The aging process of all things living and non-living involves change. People, animals, plants, buildings, cars and clothes all show the wear of aging so to think we are protecting our personal security by a knee-jerk resistance to change is an illusion. Sometimes we must change our habits, lifestyles and environments as a *matter* of life and death.

Many church people say they are against "change for the sake of change" thinking such changes are unwarranted. Yet some gerontologists encourage the elderly to make changes, choosing different routes to walk or modifying the order in which they usually do things. It isn't the change that is important, but rather that they encourage physical, emotional, and cognitive flexibility, and therefore help prevent the rigidity that often develops in older people.

We live in a time when change in the church's mission is absolutely required if it is to survive because this is an era of tremendous change. To share our message effectively is the clear responsibility of the church, but if this message is to speak to our modern world in a way that is understandable and convincing. We must find a language, mode and style that fits in with the extraordinary changes that have taken place in the knowledge, technologies, cultural interests and styles of our time. This conviction lies behind most of the recommendations that are made in these discussions.

I am not alone in realizing the urgent need for church renewal. People like Bishop John Shelby Spong and John Killinger have contributed to the literature on this subject. Spong's *Why Christianity Must Change or Die!* comes from a more radically liberal theology than most of our church members would embrace. Killinger, too, sees a need for immediate action which is shown in his subtitle: *A Homiletic for the Last Days of the Church.*

Growth in numbers is not the primary objective of genuine church renewal, but obviously we do not want to downsize our churches for the wrong reasons. Kenneth Woodward, religion editor for *Newsweek*, a reliable source of information about the American church, wrote an article in 1993, "Dead End for the Mainline?" pointing out that "the mightiest Protestants are running out of money, members and meaning." He cites the huge losses sustained by major denominations: Presbyterians from 1965 to 1992 lost 1.4 million members; American Baptists, 1965-1993, 100,000; Lutherans, 1965-1992, 500,000, United Methodists, 1965-1992, 2.4 million; United Church of Christ, 1992-1995, 500,000; Episcopal, 1965-1991, 1.2 million; and Disciples of Christ, 1965-1991, 900,000.

Although a decade has passed since these numbers were compiled, in spite of hopeful signs in some quarters, mostly this rate of decline continues. The United Methodist Church reports the losses for 2004 to be 65,000. The United Methodist Church and the Presbyterian Church, U.S.A. reflect the continual shrinking of mainline churches: between 1995 and 2001, each denomination lost almost 200,000 members, some 40,000 members a year.

These losses are the result, I believe, of evangelism not being a conscious priority in the lives of our churches, plus the social and sociological changes that have taken place in our time. We need to alter our thinking. One of the most needed transformations is for more of our members to become deeply committed to the most important seven words Jesus spoke to his followers: "Go and make disciples of all nations."

2

The Great Leveler

May the God of hope fill you with all joy and peace as you trust in him, so that you may overflow with hope by the power of the Holy Spirit (Rm 15:13).

Besides the most basic of the church's ministries – presenting the call to and the opportunity for a personal relationship with God – perhaps the greatest contribution it has made throughout its history has been its providing people with the capacity to respond to their experiences, even adverse ones, in positive ways. If it were not for the church's message, the world would be virtually void of this option. With few exceptions, those outside the church's influence are unaware of any alternative to reacting to life's sufferings, problems and anxieties except to endure them as best they can. When a person can grasp the awareness that all adverse experiences can be looked on positively, they discover there is dependable and inspiring hope regardless of what they are facing at a given time.

The Christian view of adversity is such a Rubicon of practical value for facing life's problems I often wonder how those who are not privy to it can maintain their sanity, or how any of us were ever able to live with any degree of peace of mind before the tools of Christian positive thinking were put in our hands. Any Christian life and thought that becomes available to us is of course due in some way to the ministry of the church. For instance, those who have benefitted immeasurably from reading the Bible but have never been active participants in the life of any church often do not realize that the Scriptures are themselves a ministry of the church. All the New Testament documents were written by early members of the church, and we would not have the Bible had the church not carried it over the ages to every generation in every continent and culture.

To be sure, many secular admonitions encourage positive thinking, but a genuinely hope-filled response to suffering is impossible without faith in a transcendent power. If there is no one who manages our experiences beyond ourselves, there can be no assurance that our problems will have positive solution.

The one exception to this rule is a courageous endurance that tenaciously refuses to allow suffering to yield to despair. But while this attitude is commendable, it is hardly positive. In order to feel positive about adverse experiences, we must believe, or at least hope, that rewarding experiences that are more than worth the suffering will someday come to us. This is precisely the message of Jesus Christ to the church.

My confidence that believing rich blessings will come to those who trust, as best they can, in this principle of faith has come from some of the church's insightful teachers. It is one of those biblical gems that seem to be right before our eyes after we see them but elude us until we come to the moment when our eyes have been opened to them. For most of us these truths cannot be seen until someone shows them to us, and often it has been a committed servant of the church who uncovers for us these hitherto hidden mysteries in Scriptures.

Often this biblical truth is hidden and so many active church people just don't perceive these "little feasts" that come only to the hungry. Unfortunately, without severe suffering or desperation, most people do not become "hungry" enough to find them. They simply cannot believe that by trusting in God, even with a trust that is accompanied by doubts, the suffering we experience will lead to rich and joyous experiences. Yet this is the amazing teaching of the Christian church. There are countless Christians who would be delivered of mountains of distress and worry if they took the Bible's teachings on this subject at its word.

For years I thought Jesus was speaking with something akin to Eastern symbolic hyperbole until I was led to see that he meant exactly what he said. If we try – and try is the operative word here – to give God's kingdom our ultimate concern, the highest priority in our lives, all of our basic needs such as food, clothing and housing, will be met in abundance: "But seek first his kingdom and his righteousness and *all* these things shall be yours as well" *(Mt 6:33)*.

When I first pondered this passage, I was struck with the incomparable resource it promised. But however wonderful such a storehouse of "all these things" would be, it might as well not have existed for I knew I was as far from being able to put God's kingdom first as Saddam Hussein was from receiving the Nobel Peace Prize. Then came the day when one of those sterling, unsung teachers of the church and its Book pointed out to me that Jesus had not insisted that I put God's kingdom and his righteousness first. He had said that "all these things" would come to me if I would only *try, seek*, to put them first. What a difference this insight has made in my life in making the greatest of all resources accessible to me. As long as I make a reasonable and sincere effort to put the way of God first in my life, I will never go without having life's basic needs met.

After living for a time with this priceless promise, experiencing its fulfillment time and again, I came to see that our basic needs include important ones we usually forget about. Our heavenly Father surely knows our lives cannot be too meaningful without recreation and friends and romance and special celebrations and professional accomplishments, to name a few. God is not at all stingy with these, nor does God insist those who pursue God's kingdom live in a shack, wear only well-worn clothes, and eat bread and water. God knows full well some of life's "extras" are actually basic needs for us, and God loves to give good gifts to us. "If you then, who are evil, know how to give good gifts to your children, how much more will your Father in heaven give good things to those who ask him" *(Mt 7:11)*.

We must remember, as Luke's version of this statement shows, that God's best gifts are not things at all. They are spiritual, whereas material things are destined to run dry of meaning. "If you then, who are evil, know how to give good gifts to your children, how much more will the heavenly Father give the Holy Spirit to those who ask him" *(Lk 11:13)*. It is an idea that does not sell too well in post-modern America, but we would enjoy a far greater national culture and life if the spiritual experience and power were placed above material things. That seldom happens in this country, but if materially wealthy people do not make use of this spiritual reality, inevitably there comes a time when they would give everything they have for the serenity and security that only the Spirit can bring.

The church's most formative teacher, the Apostle Paul, was quite clear about the literalness of Jesus' promise, even though it might seem so much "foolishness" to those who's eyes are still blind to it: "We know that all things work together for good for those who love God, who are called according to his purpose" *(Rm 8:28)*. What a claim! "Everything" means nothing, no situation, or condition of suffering, or any adversity lies outside the effective application of this amazing promise. As unbelievable as it seems, those who seriously act on this promise find it is consistently kept.

Paul tells us he "learned" this preëminent truth in the most difficult of times, chained to a Roman guard 24 hours a day, yet he sets it down as a seminal principle of his life and faith: "Not that I complain of want; for I have learned, in whatever state I am, to be content" *(Ph 4:11)*. It was possible for Paul to be profoundly confirmed in this cardinal rule of trusting in the abiding care of his Lord, and he urges his readers to consciously trust that God in Christ will bring every adversity they face to personal victory, promising that it will be made relatively insignificant by the anticipation of the coming fulfillment of blessing.

Many in the church fail to appropriate this great promise as an extraordinarily valuable and practical tool for the faith community because there is a widespread misunderstanding of the word "faith." The common misconception of the word's meaning sees faith and belief as synonymous, especially in English-speaking cultures. This leaves people with the problem of getting from not believing in God's caring for us to believing in it. Many come to this belief in a very direct way. They are just able to accept this faith at some point without doubting it, but for others who cannot seem to come to faith by that route, it is the "what to do" of faith that is so important.

The critical need in our congregations is for clarification that faith is initially and essentially *trust* and not belief, as we normally use the word. One's initial act of trust in God leads one to belief in God, but belief is not faith's initial act. For those who come to genuine faith in Christ with an experience of repentance and grace, there is no need to explain "what to do" to begin a personal relationship with Christ, but those who are not given this marvelous occurrence need to know there is another way.

Believing is a function of the mind. In order to come to believe in something one has not previously believed in, there must be evidence, which is precisely what is missing when it comes to believing in God, or in Jesus as the Christ. This is the impossible "Catch-22" if faith is the same as belief: We cannot hear the Good News of God's reconciling love for us until we believe in it, and we cannot believe in it until we hear it.

But when faith is seen as essentially trust, there is a way we can move from unbelief to belief. When we encounter the invitation of Jesus Christ to re-creation and reconciliation, having no evidence to convince us, we cannot at the outset believe in it. We are then at the crucial juncture of *unfaith* and faith: If we are ever to come to believe, we must first decide to trust. Responding to the Gospel in faith is initially a decision, the decision to trust in Jesus Christ.

The act of faith is not only initially trust, it is also mainly and primarily trust because it retains the character of trust in the ongoing relationship between us and God. A personal, caring relationship cannot be maintained without the dynamic of trust remaining active in the relationship. When the Gospel comes to us, it is first and foremost a Person whom we encounter. A relationship of any depth with a person requires trust. Our initial relationship with God made possible by our decision to trust God, takes on belief as it encounters the mounting evidence of an incomparably more meaningful life for us in a personal relationship with the Savior and Lord of the Gospel. But trusting in Christ always remains more basic than belief. However much we believe in someone, we cannot retain a personal relationship with that person if we stop trusting him or her.

So faith is available to anyone. It is the "great leveler" of access to God. Not everyone can believe in God to begin with, but anyone, regardless of their intelligence or moral character can decide to trust God, whether or not they believe in God. They decide to try. (The intimate relationship between trusting and trying is interesting.) Trusting is in fact a form of trying, even if belief is not there yet. It is a trusting in God in order to see if God is for real. We trust precisely because we do not believe, and the initial decision to trust God leads us through personal experiences to the other meaning of the word: When we sincerely try to live as though there is a loving God, we come to trust God in the sense of having confidence in God's unwavering care for us. This is believing at its best.

This understanding of faith needs to be far more widely disseminated throughout the church, and in turn by the church to people outside its fellowships. Because of my own use of this understanding of faith repeatedly in efforts to help people come to a personal relationship with God in Jesus Christ, I am convinced the church's evangelism would be far more effective if this concept of faith were more widely understood and shared with people outside its ranks. There are countless people in the world who do not believe in God, or who do not believe they can have a right relationship with God, because they are simply not aware that they can begin a close friendship with God by deciding to trust God regardless (no comma) of their doubts.

Anyone who is living without a conscious, practical trusting in God is facing all the challenges and problems in life without being equipped with the most effective spiritual tool imaginable. Anyone who is not blessed with the confidence or hope in the promise that God will bring rich rewards out of any suffering or problem is missing out on inestimable peace of mind and joyous anticipation. I cannot imagine any worldly knowledge that could rival these two principles of faith for banning spiritual doubts and anxiety from our lives. They deserve the church's clear and constant emphasis in its teaching of its members and in its witness to the world.

It is a great blessing to live in the age of positive thinking. Pastors, teachers and evangelists who have the most divergent and conflicting ways of viewing Christian faith see the value and power of positive thinking through the same eyes. Prominent spokespersons for the church in our time from preachers like Norman Vincent Peale to Jimmy Swaggart, Robert Schuller and Yongi Cho, who would hardly think of themselves as holding kindred theological views, all share the same emphasis on positive thinking. This concept has been in the wings of the church in many ways but in the last few decades it has taken center stage.

This truth is as appealing and accessible to the uneducated as it is to the academic. It is a vital tool for simple church folk, but many intellectuals also "come to the manger" to honor this child of our time.

I find it interesting that in our era psychologists beat us by almost a century in stressing positive attitudes and their practical preëminence for peace of mind and happiness, yet the value of positive thinking was emphasized in Scripture millennia before our modern gurus began to promote it. Remember Paul's statement? "Finally, beloved, whatever is true, whatever is honorable, whatever is just, whatever is pure, whatever is pleasing, whatever is commendable, if there is any excellence and if there is anything worthy of praise, think about these things *(Ph 4:8)*.

Both church people and scientists could have had this tool at their disposal much earlier if they had taken it literally when they read it in the Scriptures. The reason for church's neglect in this case remains a mystery for me, but the Bible is often the last place scientists and other intellectuals look for truth. In fact, it's worse; in most cases they don't get to the Bible at all. Much of this aversion is due, I'm sure, to fundamentalists' claim of the Bible as being "inerrant," which is a pernicious and absurd view that is naturally off-putting to any intellectually inclined person.

In any event, this is just another way God has "hidden these things from the wise and the intelligent and have revealed them to infants" *(Lk 10:21)*. And rather than be critical of intellectuals who don't consult the Scriptures, we would do well to take on the attitude Jesus showed, being thankful "these things" are accessible to the intellectually unsophisticated. This verse tells us "Jesus rejoiced in the Holy Spirit and said,... yes, Father, for such was your gracious will."

The unique utility of positive thinking is rooted in the structure God created for our minds, particularly the dynamics between its subconscious and conscious levels. In spite of differences and disagreements between various schools of psychology, there seems to be unanimity about the subconscious. Most psychologists agree there is a storage level of the mind and we are not conscious of much of its contents at any given time. When we speak of the subconscious, with whatever name we give it, we are actually talking about our memories. We have memories of which we are not consciously aware until something happens to trigger them into our conscious minds. Nevertheless these stored memories influence our attitudes and reactions and program the ways we think about ourselves and the ways we react to our experiences, even when we are not consciously in touch with them. Our self-concept, our peace of mind, and much of our basic self-confidence are largely determined by them.

In living with our subconscious memories, we do not have to remain passive puppets. God has not left us without means of changing our programming. Simple repetition is the key to our deliverance from our heartless, rote, subconscious commander. By constantly repeating positive thoughts, responses, and the images of ourselves we want to have, at some point these overtake the negative storage that has previously determined our attitudes and behavior. Repetition got us there in the first place and by persistently practicing repetition in our thoughts and words and behavior we can eventually replace them by positive thinking.

Unlike the conscious mind, the subconscious does not have any mechanism for editing what is stored in its memory. The conscious is the data on our "screens" at the moment, the subconscious is the "hard drive" of the human computer, which stores whatever we tell it. It does not consider the accuracy or moral rectitude of the data. Whatever it hears, it retains in its memory.

I have counseled a number of women, for instance, who were very attractive physically but were convinced they were ugly. (I have not encountered this problem in men, perhaps because our society does not place as high a priority on physical attractiveness for men as it does for women.) For whatever reason, something they had been told or experienced caused them to tell their subconscious they were unattractive. Those who have poor self images do not derive their low self esteem from the actual facts about themselves, thus people who are physically, mentally or intellectually deformed or deficient can have very positive self images because they do not think of themselves in terms of their negative characteristics, but have formed self images from internalized positive impressions. So negative self images can be replaced by the repetition of positive ones that we finally internalize.

I have found by assigning to counselees who have low self esteem or inferiority feelings the task of making lists citing all the good things about themselves and their lives they can think of and then repeating aloud these positives a number of times every day, then amazing transformations do take place with those who take the assignment seriously, often within days or in a *matter* of weeks.

One young woman thought she was unattractive physically and lacking in any special ability, which was a concept she had of herself for which there was no valid reason. I tried to point out to her that in fact her looks were quite extraordinary and she was quite gifted. For one thing, she could make quick, amazingly accurate pencil drawing renditions of people or objects. But nothing I said convinced her. Since her self image was a result of having negative input imbedded in her consciousness, now she needed to store new positive data about herself. I suggested she repeat positive affirmations about herself slowly and emphatically some 20 times twice daily with her eyes closed. Her view of herself did not change immediately, but in several weeks a more positive self concept began to take root. It took more than six months, but it was soon obvious that she had divested herself of the negative self image that had poisoned her peace of mind for years. In our last session she smiled broadly and said, "This really worked wonderfully. I now realize I am the most beautiful and most talented woman in the world!" She was kidding, of course.

I know of no other therapeutic method that is as effective as this one for changing negative impressions of ourselves. This application of positive thinking is one of the most extraordinary gifts God has given to the creatures he has made in his own image. As effective and valuable as this method is for changing our attitudes and feelings about ourselves, it is still unknown to many Christians. This positive affirmation tool needs to have far wider dissemination by the church.

3

Positively Wrong

But speaking the truth in love, we must grow up in every way into him who is the head, into Christ (Eph 4:15).

Hopefully I have made the point that positive thinking is supremely valuable for the Christian life. But it is also important that we understand what positive thinking is not, because there is a widespread notion about positive thinking among church people, especially denominational officials and staff people, that we should not speak in negative terms about anything being wrong with the church. This attitude might be amusing, if it were not also one of the main problems in contemporary church life. Even discussing this book project with clergy colleagues often elicits a response like, "Are you sure you want to say what's wrong with the church? That sounds so negative."

This could very well be a reaction to unconstructive negative criticism that tends to be so debilitating in church circles. Too often, however, this reaction simply puts the church in a denial mode. Most of us have experienced those in our churches who undermine the spirit of unity and joy by constantly expressing negative or inappropriate sentiments. But this should not preclude our correcting misguided attitudes or practices in the church. An unwillingness to hear criticism places us in a stance that impedes valid reform efforts. Granted, it is often advisable to couch criticisms in positive ways, but we should not play silly word games or trivialize the situation when we are trying to address serious failings in the lives and ministries of our churches.

The Biblical conception of faith requires a pattern of positive thoughts and behavior. This does not mean we can never make any criticism or admit there is anything wrong in our church's life or ministry. The Christian faith is big on honesty. So the true Christian attitude is not that we refuse to face our problems, or that we pretend they don't exist; it is rather that regardless of any problem we might face, God will bring a solution to it, if we trust God. Many in our churches get uncomfortable when criticism is voiced against their church or denomination. This may intimidate others in the church from correcting wrongs.

Genuine positive thinking, on the other hand, says anything negative can be overcome by God who is working through us. Again, it does not refuse to acknowledge anything negative. Sound positive thinking requires we squarely face our problems and seek solutions with a confident trusting that God will help us through them. A positive attitude sees problems clearly, but looks confidently beyond them to working them out. Christians with genuinely positive attitudes can see beyond immediate negative experiences with hope and trust, but they do not deny that negative realities exist nor try to discourage paying attention to them.

The practice of discouraging any criticisms of "the church" is tantamount to a contemporary heresy. The word heresy, like apostasy, has largely fallen out of usage in the church because its connotation would seem to require harsh, inquisitional methods. It implies a judgmental stance with which we are no longer comfortable. But a heresy is simply a way of thinking that scholars and church leaders have deemed dangerously wrong.

Certainly there are certain beliefs and practices today which are seriously wrong. In fact, the unwillingness to point out behaviors as unchristian when the consensus of the church's responsible thinkers deem them so serves to prevent the correction of such errors. The seminal conviction we have inherited from the great reformers is that the church needs to be "always reforming." This alone should prompt us to address theological, ecclesiastical, liturgical, ethical and moral errors vigorously. Obviously, a climate where church folk feel intimidated from verbalizing criticisms is one where reform will not be welcomed.

This stance also promotes a superficial kind of "niceness" in our churches where under a pleasant surface layer there lie many frustrations and annoyances. It might appear to be all "sweetness and light" permeated with corporate Christian love, but too often it is actually a type of repression. So actually this contemporary "heresy" has two immoral dimensions: it is not only repressive, it is also hypocritical.

How such a reaction to criticism could develop in the church founded by Jesus of Nazareth is odd indeed. The church would not have come into being if Jesus had approached errors and failures this way. He pulled no punches in criticizing the practices of the "church" leaders of his time. Remember this one? "You brood of vipers. How can you speak good things, when you are evil? For out of the abundance of the heart the mouth speaks" *(Mt 12:34)*. Or this one? "You blind guides. You strain out a gnat but swallow a camel. Woe to you, scribes and Pharisees, hypocrites. For you clean the outside of the cup and of the plate, but inside they are full of greed and self-indulgence" *(Mt 23:24-25)*.

This preacher of the most positive message and ministry in history could not have been also history's reformer par excellence had he shrank from bringing every error and idolatrous religious practice into the blazing light of the most scalding utterances ever pronounced in Israel's prophetic history.

Jesus' "in your face" preaching was not a radical departure from his prophetic history. Direct and blistering pronouncements were frequent in that tradition. Israel's prophets encouraged and inspired their people with unforgettable balms of comfort and hope, but they often also struck at the religious and moral lapses of their people with candid and brutal frankness. They frequently incurred such violent reactions to their chastisements that they were imprisoned and killed. The Jews treatment of their prophets brought on some of Christ's harshest pronouncements. He did not let his hearers forget this shameful blight on their ancestry.

So caustic were Jesus' comments on this subject he declared his contemporaries would reap the awful judgment of God for what their forebears had done to the prophets: "Woe to you. For you build the tombs of the prophets whom your ancestors killed. So you are witnesses and approve of the deeds of your ancestors; for they killed them, and you build their tombs. Therefore also the Wisdom of God said, 'I will send them prophets and apostles, some of whom they will kill and persecute,' so that this generation may be charged with the blood of all that was shed since the foundation of the world, from the blood of Abel to the blood of Zechariah, who perished between the altar and the sanctuary. Yes, I tell you, it will be charged against this generation" (Lk 11:47-51).

The Bible would be a vastly different and far less helpful source if it adhered to the silly standard of "positive" expression that has become the bane of ecclesiastical correctness in our churches today. Although there is a cadre of vigorous voices who assail the church's tragic deficiency of prophetic preaching in our time, the tendency to discourage of criticism is due to our fatally flawed need to be nice. We will not see a strong surge of prophetic, reforming proclamation and witness in the church until this intimidating influence is effectively counteracted.

All right-thinking Christians know the church is made up of sinners, thus the need for ongoing reformation in the church. We know there are errors and shortcomings so any attempt to quiet critical comments amounts to organizational dishonesty and repression. In our personal lives we would avoid at all costs a physician who tried to treat our medical disorders without first diagnosing them. Accurate diagnosis is an absolute requirement for effective treatment, and such diagnosis may not be "positive." So it is with problems and errors in the church. As uncomfortable as addressing them may be, they must be diagnosed by those committed to progress and reform.

A widespread discouragement of critical appraisals in the church has kept it repeating countless errors and ineffective patterns. It is an abdication of responsibility that has serious ramifications for the future, for we are burdening the faith community of the future with inflexible traditions. There is a stringent responsibility on church leaders of every age to insure, as well as they can, that for the duration of their stewardship the church will remain in sensitive and aggressive readiness to make whatever changes renewal would require. The current clergy and church leaders hold the keys to the quality of the church's future, either leaving a legacy of continually renewing openness or a frozen, closed and deadening "pleasantness."

Scriptures indicate God has a particularly fierce judgment against any set of wrong beliefs and practices that get formed into a tradition. "You abandon the commandment of God and hold to human tradition.... You have a fine way of rejecting the commandment of God in order to keep your tradition" (Mk 7:8-9). Unfortunately the malpractice of God's people adversely affects not only current participants but countless others in ages to come. The longer we allow this petty positiveness to continue, the more we carry to its future members a "gagged" church, increasingly resistant to renewal.

Perhaps the most detrimental aspect of this current behavior is that it militates against renewal in general. It's part of our human nature. When any institution, agency, group, or family intimidates its members into repressing rather than expressing their critical sentiments, they will soon learn to keep valuable suggestions to themselves.

I once heard my son tell his grandfather he was wrong about something. I told him he had been disrespectful and shouldn't criticize his grandfather. Later our family took a short car trip. When we got to a restaurant for lunch, Dad caught his jacket in the car door as he was getting our of the car, but I didn't notice it until I saw him trying to dislodge it. As we were walking away from the car my son whispered to me he had seen his grandfather close the door on his jacket. I asked, "Well, why in the world didn't you tell him?" After a moment of staring at me with a childlike look of confusion, he replied, "I thought you said I shouldn't ever tell Granddaddy he did anything wrong."

Adolf Hitler was once adored by many German people as a charismatic savior, "Fuhrer." When he first came to power, he received truckloads of letters making suggestions for the new government. When the laws that banned as subversive all pronouncements against his government were passed, Hitler was heard to bemoan the fact that people had stopped writing to him with their suggestions. Since criticism is implied even in every positive suggestion, it follows we will be discouraged from making suggestions when we are discouraged from making criticisms.

An unfailing characteristic of life is expression. The higher the life form the more expressive it is. It is more than a coincidence that what we consider the highest form of life is referred to as the Word. The most notable distinction between plants and animals is that plants, so far as we can discern, have no means of expression. By discouraging expression, we reduce the depth and vibrancy of life. The more we quell free expression, the more we make the church a closed, brittle and empty corporate wineskin into which new wine cannot be poured.

Many times the verbal walls of the church have stiffened into an inflexibility similar to what happens with aging skin when life goes out of it and its texture changes from a supple resilience to a brittle rigidity. The more this happens in the church, the less it can hold the dynamic fermentation of new ideas. Jesus was quite clear about this: "No one puts new wine into old wineskins; otherwise, the wine will burst the skins, and the wine is lost, and so are the skins; but one puts new wine into fresh wineskins" (Mk 2:22).

Renewal is many things, but it is more the infusion of new life than anything else, and new life cannot thrive long in infertile soil. It's a law of life: life forms require sharing their soil in order to have rich fertility. Recently botanists have emphasized biodiversity, claiming if trees are to remain healthy, they must have plants other than trees in their environments. Christians who want the church to be vibrant and alive must insure it has optimum opinion, as well as racial and cultural, diversity. Such an imperative is based on their own self-interest as much as their commitment to compassion, altruism and mission. Like trees, if we do not share our Christian fellowship with people who perceive the church, its faith and its mission differently from the way we perceive them, our own spiritual health suffers severely. We might be able to retain our Christian faith and our commitment to its church without diversity, but it will soon become far less exciting, interesting and joyful. In fact, it will soon be lifeless.

Could this be why so many new Christians enter the church with enthusiasm and excitement but soon grow cool and complacent about it? New Christians can provide us with a therapeutic method for dealing with our own spiritual dullness. Several times I have watched longstanding church members who have lost the vital edge of their faith encounter new Christians who are excited about their "new life." In the process, the new inspire the apathetic, helping them recover their own spiritual vitality. It doesn't even have to be new Christians who have this effect on us. The same inspiration can come when we find ourselves among Christians from different backgrounds, different races, cultures, nationalities, or even different levels of society.

I once served as interim pastor of a church that had a Korean congregation associated with it. Soon I felt a renewed interest and enjoyment in my Christian faith and life through my association with the Korean Christians, especially with their pastor and his family. Because they were so excited about their faith, I "caught it from them." When I was with this pastor I could always sense some of his enthusiasm invading my feelings, and when I was with his congregation in a worship service or a time of fellowship, I would always leave saying to myself something like, "I would really love to be with Christians like these much more often."

Since, as noted, we indirectly discourage voicing all sentiments when we discourage the expression of critical sentiments, we act against our own spiritual interests when we do it. We lose the benefits (and they are often incalculable benefits) of all that others might have to offer us when we dampen their efforts to verbalize critical opinions and points of view. And we sometimes lose not only what they have to offer; we lose the people themselves. Every now and again I come across Christians who have finally given up and left their church because they have repeatedly been denied the opportunity to express themselves.

What makes this all the more lamentable is that most of these Christians have been extraordinarily gifted people. Surely we ought to realize that when we reject people's expressions, we reject the people themselves. That is invariably the way it feels. It's not too much to ask for us to remember this because we are all that way: When our expressions are rejected, we feel we have been rejected, and it cuts close to the very essence of Christianity that we should of all things not reject people.

Have you noticed that when very gifted people are rejected, it tends to be the most mediocre or less gifted ones who do the rejecting? They feel it is in their interest to do this. I've seen this many times, and it is a sorry state of affairs that cripples the church in countless ways. Some church or denominational group will have been taken over by people who perceive they must protect their standing among their colleagues or church members. They do this by minimizing the opportunity for highly gifted people to express themselves or become actively involved in the leadership of the group. Of course this happens in every arena of human affairs: business, education, government, community-volunteer efforts, and other contexts where people work together. Our world would be a better place if the most intelligent, most talented, and most gifted people were encouraged in the maximum use of their strengths and abilities.

I once served in a Presbyterian U.S.A. presbytery where I met a retired chaplain who also served a church in that presbytery. He had been a full colonel in the army and had been administrator of religious activities for large bases, and supervised sizeable staffs of chaplains and chaplains' assistants. After getting to know him, I kept wondering why he was not put in more responsible positions in the organization. He was supremely talented and worked with people and their interpersonal problems with as much skill and ability as I had ever seen; but he was kept in subsidiary roles where he was not in "competition" with those who had carved out their niches of leadership over a period of time.

The ministry committee in that organization was widely known throughout the churches it represented for its amazing, often laughable, incompetence, (That was where several pastors were appointed to the special committee for evangelism that I mentioned, none of whom had ever shown the slightest gift or interest in evangelism.), but the retired chaplain was never asked to serve on that committee. I suggested to him that he was eminently qualified to serve on the committee he should allow himself to be nominated to it. He said he had expressed interest in being put on it several times, but he was never asked or put forward by the nominating committee. Why was such a qualified man not asked to serve in such a leadership vacuum?

Looking around that denominational organization, I noticed two things: the leaders demonstrated a consistent and "pleasant" ineffectiveness, and they consistently avoided selecting the most competent to lead in the various areas of service. There were prominent, successful business leaders active in that presbytery's churches, for instance, but those chosen to lead its stewardship committee had no notable experience in finances at all. Later the organization got into rather stringent financial trouble. Surprise!

There were also competent scholars, one who had published a book that won much acclaim in theology, and another who had studied in one of Europe's most highly regarded theological schools, whose scholarly expertise was quite evident, and who also had written a very commendable book. When a program of training for lay pastors was developed, neither of these two was asked to serve in the planning of it or teaching in it. When I pointed this out to several people in the organization, they, too, were aware of the pattern, but when I mentioned the problem to anyone in the leadership of the presbytery, I got a "you're being negative" look. I finally quit trying.

I'm sure these leaders would vigorously deny any overt discrimination, and some of them were probably not even aware of it. It is often insidiously subtle, as is the case of a host of other destructive behaviors. It would be helpful if mature people could understand that if race, culture, sex, and age discrimination are so wrong, discrimination against talent and expertise surely is as well. Leaders with this attitude, however, are not nearly as interested in what is best for the church as they are about what is best for themselves. We all know this does not occur in just a few isolated cases; it exists throughout the church. Only God knows what we could accomplish if we could set aside jealousies and competitions and use our most gifted people for the tasks, problems and challenges of the church's life and ministries.

I hasten to add that there is nothing wrong with being mediocre or not being highly gifted. The church would have serious problems if all the Christians of average or below average abilities stopped serving. Many times there are no highly talented folk to take on the responsibilities. There is nothing wrong with not having been endowed with extraordinary talents, but there is something very wrong about keeping those with ability from serving. And the seriousness of this practice is heightened because it directly hinders God's intentions for his people. When those with gifts and talents are kept from serving, it should make us tremble. For it is God who gifted them with the intention of doing God's work in the church.

> To one is given through the Spirit the utterance of wisdom, and to another the utterance of knowledge according to the same Spirit, to another faith by the same Spirit, to another gifts of healing by the one Spirit, to another the working of miracles, to another prophecy, to another the discernment of spirits, to another various kinds of tongues, to another the interpretation of

tongues. All these are activated by one and the same Spirit, who allots to each one individually just as the Spirit chooses" *(1 Co 12:8-11).*

For what purpose are these gifts given to people?

The gifts he gave were that some would be apostles, some prophets, some evangelists, some pastors and teachers, to equip the saints for the work of ministry, for building up the body of Christ *(Eph 4:11-12).*

Those who encourage a climate of "mushy" positiveness in order to deny people the honest expression of their gifts should remember, "It is a fearful thing to fall into the hands of the living God" *(Heb 10:31).* I have come to believe wholeheartedly in the spiritual principle that "what goes around comes around." I see it as a rephrasing of "Vengeance is mine, and recompense, for the time when their foot shall slip; because the day of their calamity is at hand, their doom comes swiftly" *(Dt 32:35).*

I can think of no better way for a loving God to bring home to those who discourage fellow Christians from using their gifts than to give them a dose of their own medicine. God loves them, too, and is no autocratic dictator, but Scriptures tell us that God disciplines us as any loving parent would *(Heb 12:7ff).* God does not punish to inflict pain on others for "just desserts," but rather that God's children might change their uncaring ways. Suffering is one way to get the attention of the recalcitrants quickly and to discourage them from inflicting rejection on others now that they've felt God's favor fade away.

I am cognizant that my own life experiences of repression and rejection, which all people suffer to greater or lesser degrees, have brought me to this keen empathy for those who go through similar waters, and I trust they have made me careful not to do likewise to those around me who are trying to use their gifts for God's glory. We must also recognize it is the church that has brought to our world the most profound and significant concept ever introduced into human history.

This was impressed on me when I attended a lecture given by Paul Tillich at Harvard in 1964 when I was a graduate student at the Divinity School. Several years before that he had left Harvard to teach at the University of Chicago, but returned to campus to give the lecture I was privileged to hear. I'll never forget the point he made, that the concept of *agape*, unconditional love, is a unique contribution of Jesus. The world knew nothing of this most significant and valuable insight for human relations before Jesus proclaimed it, and it has been the Christian church that has been the historic bearer of this concept. We hear it often mentioned in contexts far removed from church. It is no doubt the most widely talked about concept the Christian faith has contributed to the world, yet few recognize that Jesus of Nazareth was the author of it. Unconditional love, of all Christian values, is the crown jewel of ethics and human relations, and it is this value that is violated by any who repress the concerns of their fellow church members.

We also ought not lose sight of how failing to love unconditionally affects a church's witness and influence outside its fellowship. How can we expect to be loving examples to the world the way the early Christians were if we conduct the church's affairs with repression in the guise of "positive attitudes"? Or how can we urge those outside the church to treat one another with dignity, democracy, and openness if we do not encourage free expression and participation in the life of the church. "I give you a new commandment, that you love [agape] one another. Just as I have loved you, you also should love one another. By this everyone will know that you are my disciples, if you have love for one another" *(Jn 13:34-35)*.

This is certainly what really *matters*, and also it is clear it is one of the things that is the *matter with the church*.

4

A Strange Word

He must hold firm to the sure word as taught, so that he may be able to give instruction in sound doctrine and also to refute those who contradict (Tt 1:9).

Any assessment of the condition of the church must include the consideration of its stewardship of right thinking and behavior. One of the church's ministries that has been so valuable for its members and the world is its provision down through the ages of strong and dependable guidelines for faith and conduct. For centuries the church has made available to its people clear standards for right beliefs, right attitudes, right ethical and moral decisions, and right behavior. The world would be inestimably worse off had it not been for this kind of guidance from the church.

Throughout human history the church has been the Noah's Ark of spiritual and moral guidance. Nowhere else can people go for the direction needed to distinguish between right and wrong beliefs and living. Some of our churches are still refreshing citadels of such wholesome guidance, but it is obvious that any fair assessment would conclude that there are all too few of them.

Most families have at least one thing they don't talk about. The extended church family has some things from its biblical past that we now think were intellectually and morally very embarrassing. Time and again, during my 50 years in the ministry, I have seen how our keeping secrets in the closet has weakened the church's effectiveness in countless ways. Our desperation to avoid them shows, as do all instances of repression and denial, that we are afraid and embarrassed to face them.

When Lyndon Johnson was majority leader of the United States Senate, he was asked by a newly elected senator for his suggestions for putting together a staff for his office. Johnson said, "Before you hire anybody, you need to set down some staff rules."

"Rules? Do you have to have rules?" the new senator asked.

Johnson replied, "If you don't have fences, you don't know when the cows are out."

It seems to me we have no firm "fences" for the ethical, moral, and theological thinking and behavior of the members of our churches. This lack has wreaked havoc on the church's ability to provide solid guidelines for right thinking and behavior. We don't even like the sound of the word our classical church forebears used for it – *apostasy*. Mention it in church circles, particularly among clergy, and see what reaction you get. It will most likely be similar to the response you would get if you said you had just had a theological conversation with an extraterrestrial. "Apostasy" has long since fallen out of our "church speak."

Why is this such a strange word to us.

Actually, apostasy is not a biblical word and does not appear in any translation, but its meaning, "falling away from the truth," frequently appears in Biblical literature. Surely there is truth in the Christian faith from which it is possible to depart, and it would be foolish to think otherwise. There are right and wrong ways for Christians to believe, think and behave.

It is not that we do not believe there are any definite rights and wrongs for members of our churches. We intuitively accept traditional moral standards against lying, stealing, adultery and murder, but even for these we have no standards for holding church members accountable for the violation of them. So we have created a kind of "anything goes" climate in the church, avoiding the responsibility for dealing with members who commit moral wrongs and injustices, and justifying it with statements like, "But God loves them too," which is somehow supposed to relieve us of any effort to confront them. Volumes could be written on how God's love is used to accept wrong beliefs, attitudes and conduct.

Our subtle denial, cultivated over many years, has camouflaged this situation so as to keep it from striking us as libertarianism, but that is exactly what it is. Tragically enough, our church life and thought are therefore either "apostate" or there is no such thing. Since most assuredly there are rights and wrongs for church members, obviously apostasy is a real possibility, whether we like the sound of the word or not. If you see the contemporary church insisting on definite, clear standards of Christian truth, sexual behavior or relationships (affiliations and associations with people who are not Christians), you are looking at a different church from the one I see.

I hasten to add that I do not believe theological liberalism is the culprit. I am very proud to be a liberal. The problem to which I refer is not a self-conscious interpretation or approach at all. It is simply that we ignore these *matters*, except for a sermon on them now and then. We simply do not address these areas with any idea of identifying and promoting standards, much less insisting on compliance with them.

It is important to underscore that my theological perspective is a liberal one. If I were coming at the question of apostasy as a fundamentalist, or even as a conservative, falling away from the truth would mean something quite different from the phenomenon in the church I am referring to. I am certainly not advocating biblical literalism or a moral legalism; nor would I propose specific standards of belief, thought, and behavior that would serve as the guiding values for the church. That task would require a very diverse group of people, scholars, pastors, and lay people. I am seeking here to bear witness to the main concerns I have for the renewal of the church. What has confirmed these convictions has not been the frequent encounters I have had with the failings of the church but the many instances in which I have witnessed the church at its best.

My father had a striking gift for quick wisdom and wit. We were leaving a supermarket one morning on Miami Beach where we both lived when we met a lady with two dogs on leashes just outside the entrance to the store. Dad commented to the lady on the frenetic, feistiness of the animals. She thanked him with a definite air of pride of ownership and then remarked that although the dogs were both fox terriers, one was registered and the other was not. As we walked away from the encounter, Dad asked, "Don't registered dogs cost more than unregistered dogs?" I said I thought they usually cost a good deal more. A few steps further I queried, "Why did you ask?" He said, "Because I couldn't tell any difference."

That is an observation made by far too many outsiders about those in the church, isn't it? Even when they are people of sterling Christian character and commitment, people of the world often lack enough spiritual perception to make this unwarranted criticism. Yet many times that criticism is valid, because it perceives the vacuum of clear moral and theological codes. How can we possibly expect the world to see us any differently when we do not have clear standards? It is surely a great hindrance to effective evangelism if people outside the church cannot observe clearly distinguishable ethical and moral marks in church people. Why would people have any urgent desire to join us? Why would anyone join any organization, church, civic club, school, or group if there are no distinctive characteristics, interests, or objectives they want to share?

I would add that many moral shortcomings of church members are not instances of apostasy. A common complaint heard is that "the church doesn't do anything." This is of course patently false. The church does many things, quite a few of which are uniquely good, and quite a few that are very important ones that are not done by any other organization. Having heard this sentiment voiced many times, I finally concluded it usually refers to the lack of behavior, beliefs and opinions or church members that are distinguishable from those of people who are not active in any church. I finally figured this out from discussing their objections with a number of those outside the church. We of course cannot be impressed by opinions of those not active in church since it often is generated by their need to excuse themselves for not attending church, or from their ignorance of what actually goes on in a church.

One oft-spoken criticism you hear is, "The church is full of hypocrites." For the most part this I think is not a valid criticism. Once when I was a teenager I tried this excuse for not attending worship on my elderly pastor. His response persuaded me never again to use that one. He said, "If hypocrites are standing between you and church, they are probably closer to God than you are." There are, I'm sure, some church folk who are genuine hypocrites, but I am convinced that most of those who appear to be hypocrites are not involved in church life to deceive others but are genuinely seeking to overcome their weaknesses.

I want to reiterate that I'm not proposing a new legalism. The church has enough legalism to last for eternity. It would also be hard to find broad support for an ecumenical effort to develop a set of solid core beliefs and standards for the church. Hopefully, some day in the future such an effort can be made, because thoroughgoing church renewal must involve this effort. In the meantime, it would be entirely feasible for local churches to develop their own set of moral and theological codes, so its own members could clarify their ideas about what kinds of beliefs, thinking, and behaviors the faith community has for its members.

Those who are sincerely interested in living by Christian standards need better guidance than what the church currently offers. I believe there would be more people who would become interested in joining our churches if clearer principles or conduct, beliefs, and attitudes were set forth, and that many outside the church also would find such guidelines helpful, provided they were not legalistic.

These principles would not be laws or rules, but rather standards that would only have self-authenticating authority, which the consensus of church people would grant them at any given time. I am not advocating a comprehensive nor detailed list of orthodox values and teachings, but a set of core standards developed to deal with the most important issues that find the widest acceptance among the constituency for which they are written. Such badly needed moral and doctrinal norms are badly needed, but again they would be standards, not laws.

There does need to be a significant degree of enforcement of such standards for the church members. Mainline denominations have disciplinary procedures in place for immoral behavior on the part of clergy, but none are consistently invoked that apply to the behavior of the laity. A pastor can be disciplined by the congregation, which usually means being fired, or moved to another appointment in denominations with episcopal polity, for any number of reasons including offensive perceptions, unsubstantiated accusations, however vague or petty. Members of the congregation can treat a pastor any way they please without fear of disciplinary action by anyone, which is also true of lay people's conduct toward one another.

A contributing factor to this one-sided discipline is how committees with responsibility for oversight or consultation with pastors relate to the laity in congregations where there are problems with pastors. Panels such as the committees or boards on ministry in the mainline denominations characteristically avoid taking positions against actions taken against pastors by church members. Those who serve on these committees often seem to have little if any concern about how this approach in dealing with problematic pastoral relationships encourages an "open season" on pastors. People who engage in these attacks on pastors usually have never had anyone in authority, as limited as the authority is in congregational polity, take a clear position against lay peoples' mistreatment their actions.

The awful ordeal I went through in Connecticut, for which I have said I was primarily responsible, was made infinitely worse by the ineptness and dishonesty of two denominational staff people. Both of them were characteristic representatives of the mediocre and unimpressive denominational staff people I have referred to. I found out that the regional representative of the conference in Connecticut was saying one thing to me and the opposite to the church's committee for the pastor and congregation relations, and there was absolutely no doubt it; and the conference minister of the conference in Georgia from which I had transferred joined the fray by making absolutely false accusations against me, seemly for no reason except to make points with my mostly right wing extremist opposition in the church. There was absolutely not a shred of truth in his statements. We discovered that he even lied about the people he got the information from. We checked with all of them and they utterly denied ever having made such accusations. The treasurer of his own organization who happened to have been a friend of mine since our seminary days together, perhaps the most prominent layman in the Connecticut church, and several friends who had known me for years, including one circuit court judge, wrote to enthusiastically refute his outrageous charges. The latter's communication of these accusations abruptly ceased when my attorney wrote him a letter promising court action if these charges were repeated.

Several times I have heard clergy who serve on these committees bemoan such one-sided procedures, but they themselves refuse to adopt sanctions against obvious injustice or come out in opposition to them. The lay people who are blatantly unfair and often vicious are dealt with so tactfully they can only conclude that their actions are acceptable, or that they are not very serious, or that the difficulties were just expressions of a "bad marriage" between the pastor and the congregation.

Denominational officials and the members of these denominational committees allow the members of churches where such problems have resulted in the firing or resignation of the pastor go on into the future with the idea that everything will be rosy if they just get the right pastor. What is worse, they let the next pastor be chosen without informing him or her about what has just happened, hoping that such problems will not arise again. That is a grossly unfair way to treat the new pastor. This was clearly the case with the interim pastor who followed me in Connecticut. She resigned after a few months because of the vicious opposition she was getting in the church. She wrote me a letter to inform me of her experience when she submitted her resignation and to offer her understanding and support.

It seems the denominational committees continue to operate with this approach largely because of the force of bad tradition and quite a bit of cowardice. How could a church think such a departure from sound faith and theological and moral structures would play well with its evangelism efforts?

So though the word apostasy is a strange one to us, and almost anachronistic to the modern ear, still the idea it expresses is serious but it is treated as trivial. As bad as it may seem, for centuries we have abandoned the idea that a church can be in gross violation of New Testament standards without being called into question by any authoritative body. No *matter* how erroneous or shoddy its theology or the theology of its pastor may be, no *matter* how vacuous the theological insight and expression may be, or how unchristian its members' morality and ethics may be, those in the church do not answer to anyone regarding these *matters.* This sad state of affairs has without a doubt brought our churches to the conditions they are in today.

This has not always been the case. Many churches in the past and a few in the present have insisted on standards of belief and conduct. We have come a long way from the era when for many churches it was quite acceptable for members to be aggressively taken to task for moral and doctrinal lapses. This is largely, I'm sure, because such practices in the past were often so unduly harsh and judgmental that the church moved away from them. But to abandon setting standards for the lives of our members is equally wrong. What was needed was the far more arduous and far-reaching task of correcting the erroneous practices and the misuses of the right ones.

The New Testament clearly mandated the Christian church to be the steward and guardian of very high standards for its members.

This is not a matter of "proof texting" with isolated and unrepresentative passages. Throughout the New Testament there are many citations about reproving members who have strayed from the truth. How applicable, for instance, is the following passage to the predominant state of affairs in the church of our time?

> "I know your works; you are neither cold nor hot. I wish that you were either cold or hot. So, because you are lukewarm, and neither cold nor hot, I am about to spit you out of my mouth. For you say, 'I am rich, I have prospered, and I need nothing.' You do not realize that you are wretched, pitiful, poor, blind and naked" *(Rv 3:15-17).*

5

Leaving out the Salt

You are the salt of the earth; but if salt has lost its taste, how can its saltiness be restored? It is no longer good for anything, but is thrown out and trampled under foot (Mt 5:13).

A greater change in lives and society can hardly be imagined than what the Christian church has made throughout its mission of Christian conversion. Nothing has changed people, their morals, their priorities, their concern for others, and their experience of meaning for their lives more than the church's ministry called "new birth." It would be difficult to estimate how much worse our world would be without this incomparable stimulus.

Jesus used salt as an analogy with spiritual experience to talk about this all important "flavor" for our lives. It was such an apt metaphor that all three synoptic gospel writers included it *(Mt 5:13 Mk 9:50, Lk 14:34)*. Many foods need salt as a flavor enhancer (or in some cases a preservative). If all the ingredients in the recipe are included in the right proportions, but salt is left out, the result in many cases is a bland taste in which no cook would take pride. Thus it is so with spiritual experience. All the exterior factors can be right, church membership, participation in worship, church school, prayer, financial giving, good works, and all the rest but unless the basic spiritual experience we call the "new birth" and "conversion" is there, the "salt" is missing, and the result is a bland, powerless "religion."

Sadly, most of our churches are brimful of superficial "religious" experience. This is a problem that is impossible for church people who lack the salt to perceive, but for those who "have eyes to see," the situation is unmistakably clear, and they frequently become frustrated with the impossibility of addressing it in church circles. Too often the attitude is, "This is better than nothing," and an attempt to confront the problem is avoided. But according to Jesus, it isn't better than nothing. This kind of "unsalted" religious experience is actually of no spiritual value at all. "You are the salt of the earth; but if salt has lost its taste, how can its saltiness be restored? It is no longer good for anything, but is thrown out and trampled underfoot *(Mt 5:13)*.

The language and experience of the new birth are too often thought of in our mainline churches as belonging to other kinds of churches. But the decisive issue for the Christian life is whether or not one has a personal relationship with God, and this relationship is what is referred to as the "new birth." The main role of Jesus Christ in our spiritual experience is determined by the fact that he is Emmanuel, God with Us, as an historical *person* like us who makes it possible for us to have a *personal* relationship with God. This is the "salt" of genuine Christian experience.

This can be a very subtle *matter*. We can know about God, about everything in the Bible, the church, its worship and work, but if we do not know God personally, all of it is futile. All the other ingredients may be there, but the distinguishing "flavor" is missing. A dull, joyless church involvement usually results. This is the main problem in our churches and we will never deal effectively with its most serious problems until we address this it.

The main subject *matter* of the church is this Good News, that the Christ has made the great difference in people's lives and human society. It is the experience of conversion that has enriched the lives of families and communities, redeeming countless lives of people whose talents, contributions, and roles as caring spouses, parents, family members, and decent citizens would otherwise most probably never have been realized. Carrying this message down through the ages into the lives of people all over the world is the greatest of the church's contributions. And nothing is more inspiring and energizing for a church than to see people and families changed in this marvelous way.

Regrettably, most mainline denominational churches do not emphasize conversion. For the most part this issue is ignored. So this is the heart of the problem: conversion is what *matters* the most in the church's ministries, and this is the main thing that is the *matter* with the church. We try to proceed with our people as though they have this decisive personal experience of God when so many of them just do not, which in turn encourages their assumption that they are all right.

Again, many in the church find it difficult to confront other members—to ask if, though baptized, they have also received the "new birth". If we ask most people in the church about it, they will say they are glad to be members—and we do not want the responsibility of telling them they are wrong. Having a group or committee in our churches that seriously assesses people for membership as they did in the Early Church rather than just letting them go through the motions would be a major contribution toward renewal. But we would need to make sure this group is made up of people who have this "salt" and can perceive whether or not candidates have it before they are accepted into church membership. This would make membership in our churches mean far more than it usually does.

The greatest calamity for the modern denominational church is that conversion has been sidelined in our congregations. We are like automobile manufacturers who leave the engines out of the cars. No wonder we can't seem to get going! This is the basis for our relegating to other churches terms like the "new birth," "born again" and "saved." We are a bit too sophisticated to use such terms, but in rejecting them we reject the validity of the experience itself. Woe to us. We assume it is appropriate for us to reject this language, but this would not be such a grave omission if we used words to express the exaltation, the dazzling joy of mystic union. But the fact is that for the most part we actually do not refer to the experience at all. But for Jesus it was clearly obligatory, "You *must* be born again'" *(John 3:7)*.

The conversion experience, the new birth, is the beginning of a new and different life for the Christian, and it is a serious tragedy for those in the church who have not begun that life for it is the beginning of a life that in some way lasts forever, typically referred to in the New Testament as "eternal life." Without it our church folk are stuck in an old-death existence. With no transformation of the interior person, of their values, priorities, interests, spiritual tastes, and lifestyle so many church people are suffering from a serious spiritual blindness and have no taste for the spiritual food that nurtures and sustains their spirits. They are limited to a diet without the "flavor" and main nutrients for the eternal life in the Spirit.

The manna that comes from biblical study, Spirit preaching and prayer, plus the nurture of genuine Christian fellowship that is continually replenished for God's people is not a part of their diets. The water they drink is not the "living water" that can "spring up within us into eternal life." The millions who are not being nourished by this "bread of heaven" need our constant and passionate prayers. In profound and countless ways, they are dying. Their life is ebbing away day by day from the lack of regenerating spiritual experience and the continual life-giving nutrition it provides.

To be alive is to feel and to be dead is to have no feeling. Is not what we have said the reason there is so little "feeling" in so many of our churches? We can see it in our worship services unmistakably. There is not nearly as much feeling as you find at sports and political events. We don't need Pentecostal-type worship in our mainline denominational churches. That kind of worship would not be suitable for the religious "personalities" in most of these congregations. I have experienced powerful feeling in churches that are not Pentecostal or charismatic but are filled with people who have experienced the "new birth" and therefore hunger for and thrill to the life-giving food of Spirit preaching, Scripture, music and prayers.

Countless conferences and seminars I have attended have sought to address the need to revive evangelism in our churches. It is a constant theme of meetings for clergy and laity every year, but they seem never to deal with the essential element of the problem. Obviously what we need to do is begin by encouraging our clergy, church leaders, and teachers to strategically engage in the effort to legitimize the conversion experience in our congregations. No significant evangelism is going to take place until this is done on a large scale. There will always be numerical growth for many congregations that do not stress the "new birth" in their preaching and other ministries, but they are for the most part churches whose local population growth and demographics are favorable for such increase, but this is not evangelism. As someone has said, "We are not catching fish; we are just changing their aquaria."

We are often so familiar with truths or certain passages of scripture that we forget to ask if we are actually living by them. How about: "Jesus answered him, 'Very truly, I tell you, no one can see the kingdom of God without being born from above'" *(Jn 3:3)*?

The emphasis on the renewal of the new birth in the people and ministries of our churches is an imperative *matter* for the renewal of the church.

6

Universal Ephesus

...Paul passed through the interior regions and came to Ephesus, where he found some disciples. He said to them, "Did you receive the Holy Spirit when you became believers?" They replied, "No, we have not even heard that there is a Holy Spirit" (Ac 19:1-2).

The first schools for children, the first universities, the first orphanages, the first hospitals were creations of the Christian church. Countless people and agencies have followed its example, but with a few minor exceptions, the church was the first to provide these services to people. The church is still operating many such institutions and others are emerging in our time. Its institutional work is the most tangible of the church's achievements, but it has countless other ministries the world over. No human institution or agency has ever been able to become global except the church of Jesus Christ. Many have tried and some have extended themselves over large areas of the world, but only the Christian church has actually achieved a global reach.

I cannot see how the amazing things the church has accomplished over the years could have been done through human strength alone. Surely they are the result of the love, power and wisdom of the Holy Spirit. The work of the Holy Spirit is unarguably a vital subject *matter* of the church. I heard about a little boy who said to his church school teacher, "What I like about God is you can carry him around with you."

What greater promise has ever been made to humankind than Jesus' promise to send a Counselor who would give us reliable counsel to live by from our own inner spirit? What greater access to wisdom and guidance could we possibly have?

Yet it is appalling how many churches have grossly limited their access to the Holy Spirit. As incredible as it is, the church has too often denied itself the greatest resource possible. Is it any wonder the church instead of winning the world is losing members? It is not the primary purpose of these essays to propose measures to increase the size of the church's membership, but if the wisdom and power of the Holy Spirit were seriously, sincerely and continuously invoked, there is no telling how many more people the church would reach. Surely this is a decisive and fundamental part of what is the *matter* with the church.

When the apostle Paul went to Ephesus he found Christians there who had not experienced the baptism of the Holy Spirit. They were probably saying all the right things, but Paul perceived something vital was missing and asked them about their experience of baptism in the Holy Spirit. When they admitted their ignorance of such a thing, Paul asked further, "'Into what then were you baptized?' They answered, 'Into John's baptism.' Paul said, 'John baptized with the baptism of repentance, telling the people to believe in the one who was to come after him, that is, in Jesus.' On hearing this, they were baptized in the name of the Lord Jesus. When Paul had laid his hands on them, the Holy Spirit came upon them, and they spoke in tongues and prophesied" *(Ac 19:3-6)*.

Later we will look at the phenomenon of speaking in tongues, but for now let us consider the meaning of the situation Paul found at Ephesus as it relates to the church in our time. The idea of the Holy Spirit baptism as an additional experience to accepting Jesus Christ as personal Savior and Lord put forth by the charismatic movement has been soundly repudiated by some Christian scholars like James D.G. Dunn in his *Baptism in the Holy Spirit,* an excellent source of clarity on this issue. But our mainline Christian churches need to become far more fertile fields in which the power of the Holy Spirit can operate.

A much deeper experience with God's Spirit than most of our church people have is available to them and it is quite adaptable to mainline church life. I say this with a great deal of confidence because over 20 years ago I came to realize I needed a much stronger spiritual experience than I had in order to deal effectively with a personal crisis I was facing, so I earnestly sought a deeper Christian commitment. I was fortunate enough at that time to have God's Spirit move my relationship with God and God's kingdom to a much higher priority for me and my life changed radically. All my attitudes about spiritual *matters* and other aspects of my life were enriched incredibly. I did not become a Pentecostal or charismatic in the usual sense of those terms, but I discovered, contrary to what most mainline church people think, that a vital experience of the Holy Spirit, like other spiritual experiences and ministries, is quite adaptable to whatever religious personality we have or whatever communion to which we belong.

This should not be surprising, given that our Lord, who loves all of us beyond measure, wants as many of us as possible to receive God's blessings. It stands to reason then the Lord would give spiritual realities maximum adaptability. What I found was that I was not lacking the baptism of the Holy Spirit as was talked about in Pentecostal circles, but a true baptism of Jesus. What most of our church members have would not even qualify for the baptism of John which demands they make a serious and sincere act of repentance.

Our churches are filled, lamentably, with those who are quite short of Jesus' baptism as John the Baptist describes it. Let's not forget that John the Baptist insisted that when Jesus baptized us with the Holy Spirit and fire this authentic baptism of Jesus Christ would include the Holy Spirit's intimate presence and power in our lives. All four Gospels describe it that way. "I baptize you with water for repentance, but one who is more powerful than I is coming after me; I am not worthy to carry his sandals. He will baptize you with the Holy Spirit and fire" *(Mt 3:11)*. "I have baptized you with water; but he will baptize you with the Holy Spirit" *(Mk 1:8)*. "John answered all of them by saying, 'I baptize you with water; but one who is more powerful than I is coming; I am not worthy to untie the thong of his sandals. He will baptize you with the Holy Spirit and fire" *(Lk 3:16)*. "I myself did not know him, but the one who sent me to baptize with water said to me, 'He on whom you see the Spirit descend and remain is the one who baptizes with the Holy Spirit'" *(Jn 1:33)*.

When the Ephesians said they knew only of John the Baptist's baptism, Paul then spoke to them not of the baptism of the Holy Spirit but of the baptism of Jesus *(Ac 19:3-6)*, and when he baptized them he baptized them not in the name of the Holy Spirit but in the name of Jesus. "On hearing this, they were baptized in the name of the Lord Jesus. And when Paul had laid his hands upon them, the Holy Spirit came on them; and they spoke with tongues and prophesied. There were about twelve of them in all *(Ac 19:5-7)*.

What was missing was the baptism of Jesus. It *is* the baptism of the Holy Spirit. So those who do not have a rich and powerful experience of the Holy Spirit do not have Jesus' baptism at all. Christians, to be legitimately called that, who think they have the baptism of Jesus but have no desire for the spiritually powerful movement of his Spirit in their lives are really stuck back in John's baptism, the baptism of repentance, if they have even gotten that far!

There is a desperate need for this message to be proclaimed throughout the church, for without it we are cutting ourselves short of what our Lord came to offer us. Our baptisms as new Christians were supposed to involve the entrée of the Holy Spirit into our lives with a force like fire. Regrettably when we thought we were receiving Jesus' baptism, we actually had only gone as far as repentance. In his book *Rethinking the Church* James Emery White relates the story about a Russian comedian Yakov Smirnoff who on coming to the U.S. from Russia was unprepared for the incredible variety of instant products available in American grocery stores. He says, "On my first shopping trip, I saw powdered milk, you just add water and you get milk. Then I saw powdered orange juice, you just add water and get orange juice. And then I saw baby powder and I thought to myself, What a country!"

Sadly enough, this is the way many church members see baptism – just add water and you get a Christian. Over time baptism has been separated into two parts, and the one involving the Holy Spirit is seen as an advanced option that many church folk do not care to pursue, especially in mainline denominational churches. Many passionately reject it since they see it as a Pentecostal "extra" that is not appropriate for people in their churches. What is badly needed in our churches is thus a clearer understanding of what Christian baptism is, especially one that involves the "fire," the burning passion and witness of our Lord's Spirit.

I once heard about a church in a small farming community that caught fire and there were no resources to put it out, so people were standing around helplessly watching the church burn. A member of the church noticed a neighbor standing there who had never come to a church service and asked, "Why have you never come to our church before?"

He replied, "Your church has never been on fire before."

I'm sure the story is apocryphal, but I am convinced that many of our churches are considered "cold" because our "religion" too often lacks burning passion and power. And to me it is obvious that our evangelism is failing because the new birth and the "baptism" of Jesus are not understood and experienced, and that the healing of individuals and marriages is not happening as much as it should, not because too many people are absent from our churches, but because the Holy Spirit and fire are absent.

The "fire" Jesus mentioned no doubt refers to the power in his "baptism" that comes from the Holy Spirit. This means the mainline church for the most part is unplugged from its main power source. It goes through many of the right motions and says many of the right things, but it lacks the person and power that drive the personal, Christian conversion and effective Christian ministry, and therefore, with few exceptions, has little impact for the renewal of people's lives and communities.

There is not the slightest hope that our human words, without being transformed by the Holy Spirit into the Word of God, will change the lives of people who need desperately to be converted, no hope that broken marriages and homes will be healed, no hope that the world and its social structures will be redeemed, no hope that the kingdoms of this world will become the kingdom of God, as long as the church functions as it often does with only human power, without the salt and the fire.

Satan is another term that many mainline church people find offensive. This is not a reality with which our "sophistication" is comfortable. I don't know what your concept of Satan is. I for one cannot believe there is an actual "person" who is called Satan, but I cannot help but believe there is some malignant power, by whatever name it is called, that is opposed to God's effort to redeem God's people and the world. What more strategic blow could be struck at the ministry of a church than to distract its members from having the basic experience of a personal relationship with God and having God's Spirit empower them to resist this force of evil?

This has the marks of a conscious strategy and does not seem to be coincidental. (My favorite work on Satan is C.S. Lewis' *Screwtape Letters*. Although it does personalize Satan, it presents a comical picture of this strategy which is graphic and memorable.) Most people in the mainline churches deem the idea of Satan to be one belonging to fundamentalist and conservative theology. This I think is largely because they have always had the idea presented to them in the form of a person, which they consider intellectually unacceptable. But it strikes me that our lack of belief in the Holy Spirit's power in our lives, and our discomfort with the idea of Satan as the arch enemy of the Holy Spirit's work could very well be the primary causes of the church's inability to minister transformation and healing to people and society.

My hope is that many of us who carry the burden for the renewal of the Christian church will join in concerted and intentional prayer that our Lord will bless our efforts to develop and implement a practical strategy for opening the church to God's Spirit and work among and through God's people. Come Holy Spirit.

7

The Baby and the Bathwater

I was so intent on opposing Husserl's work that for several years I discarded all of it, including some of it that is very worthwhile (Jean Paul Sartre).

A large part of what *matters* about the church is its having been for millions of people the main source of the meaning in life. The difference between meaning and meaninglessness in life is critical, and the church through the centuries has often been its main source. This is an arena the church definitely should cling to. Why the mainline churches have to a great extent dispensed with meaning is inexplicable. In large measure we lack the spirit, the power, interest and enthusiasm people need to give meaning to their lives. For many we are seen as too reserved, too stiff, and too joyless.

We don't have to go back many years in our history to find that the more spirited characteristics of Christian faith once belonged to most of the communions in some measure. In the last 50 years, the major denominations have settled for traditional liturgies and mostly it is evangelical groups that have kept the exuberant shouting, singing, clapping and dancing – as the "Spirit" moved them. In the years before this separation began, the ministry won millions to Christ and sent missionaries all over the world.

The decline of the church's heyday began as evangelical fervor began to be considered suited only to less "sophisticated" congregations. The Pentecostal movement began growing for several decades, most likely, at least in part, to fill the vacuum left by the denominational churches. It is not inconsequential that the charismatic movement, which is characterized by a freer and more meaningful worship style, had its origin in California in a church that is perhaps the most formal and liturgical of the Protestants, where demonstrative styles of worship and ministry would be least likely practiced, a congregation of the Episcopal church.

The undeniable contribution of these congregations and their appeal is that they made worship, the Christian faith, and the Christian life interesting, exciting, and joyous to people who have found that the worship and emphases of typical denominational churches lack sufficient meaning. People in mainline denominations are turned off by the extremes they have seen or heard in the Pentecostal and charismatic churches, with the worship, ministry, and the expression of their faith by their members far too effusive for their tastes, so they reject the idea of unrestrained worship in their own churches.

But why throw out the baby with the bath water? In an effort to distinguish ourselves from these congregations because of our objection to some excesses in them, we have lost much Christian joy. I am deeply indebted to Joe Matthews and his Ecumenical Institute headquartered in Chicago in the 1960s for making many of us liberals realize we needed to get more enthusiasm in our worship. Matthews and his staff showed us we could do it and how we could do it, and the most joyful and exciting worship experiences I have ever been in were there. We clapped our hands, hit the tables with our tableware, and sang with great volume and fervor. The worship was not Pentecostal or charismatic; it was more like a "fiesta" where we discovered something we had been missing for a long time, upbeat excitement in our worship without sacrificing our liturgical heritage.

One of the great failings of the Christian church in modern and contemporary times is the lack of unity between those in radically different kinds of congregations and those in mainline denominational churches. People on each side of this divide think of those on the other as being either wrong or just "different". We have not heeded what St. Paul says on this subject:

> On the contrary, the members of the body that seem to be weaker are indispensable, and those members of the body that we think less honorable we clothe with greater honor, and our less respectable members are treated with greater respect; whereas our more respectable members do not need this. But God has so arranged the body, giving the greater honor to the inferior member, that there may be no dissension within the body, but the members may have the same care for one another. If one member suffers, all suffer together with it; if one member is honored, all rejoice together with it.
>
> Now you are the body of Christ and individually members of it. And God has appointed in the church first apostles, second prophets, third teachers; then deeds of power, then gifts of healing, forms of assistance, forms of leadership, various kinds of tongues. Are all apostles? Are all prophets? Are all teachers? Do all work miracles? Do all possess gifts of healing? Do all speak in tongues? Do all interpret? But strive for the greater gifts. And I will show you a still more excellent way.
>
> If I speak in the tongues of mortals and of angels, but do not have love, I am a noisy gong or a clanging cymbal. And if I have prophetic powers, and understand all mysteries and all knowledge, and if I have all faith, so as to remove mountains, but do not have love, I am nothing. If I give away all my possessions, and if I hand over my body so that I may boast, but do not have love, I gain nothing *(1 Co 12:22-13:3)*.

Clearly the great apostle is saying people with these gifts, the more and the less demonstrative, belong in the same church. So who are we to have relegated some of the ministry gifts that should be activated in our congregations to the more Pentecostal congregations? Old attitudes have precipitated much of the disunity that exists among Christian churches? Furthermore, in doing this we have rejected some important gifts our Lord is wanting to give the church. For all intents and purposes by doing this perhaps we have actually rejected salvation. Or at least we have made it less clear and accessible. We seldom hear those in our circles mention the most important experience the church has to offer to people, the acceptance of Jesus

Christ as savior, because we are a bit too sophisticated for such terms.

If this were just a semantic problem it would not be so bad, but it's far more than that. Not only do we not hear these terms in our churches, our members don't experience these realities. What experiences of the Christian faith are more basic and important than conversion and the power of the Holy Spirit operating in people's lives? If we wanted to use different terms to refer to these realities, that would be fine. We could find more comfortable words for them which would allow us to adapt these experiences to our congregations.

Take for instance the baptism of the Holy Spirit. Several times I have seen those who were nominal about their faith and participation in the life of the churches attend a retreat or other gathering that sought to lead them into a deeper experience and commitment to Christ, and they returned "turned on" about their faith and the ministries of their churches. Some years ago I came to see this as nothing less than the true "baptism" of Jesus, which provided the kind of relationship with Christ they should have had all along, but they had not had it before because their churches had not made clear to them what the experience should be like, and/or had not led them into it.

According to Luke's story in Acts, when Paul ministered the baptism of the Holy Spirit to the Ephesian church members (to which we referred in the previous chapter), they began to speak in unknown tongues. This may be "stretching" the exegesis, but maybe when mainline church folk experience the powerful deepening of their commitment that often takes place at spiritual retreats, the most noticeable thing about them is that they speak differently. So, too, the Ephesians began to express themselves in a totally novel way because they felt something they had never before experienced, something that could not be expressed in ordinary language.

As I said, this may be stretching what the Baptism of the Holy Spirit refers to, but I do not believe it is possible to have this deeper Christian encounter without speaking differently than we did before.

What's the Matter with the Church?

Some people are by nature more gregarious and expressive than others, but I am convinced anyone who does not show profound interest and excitement about their experience of Jesus Christ has more than likely not received his "baptism." Whether or not this burst of enthusiasm we see now and then in mainline church people is a form of "speaking in tongues," it definitely needs to happen to more of them.

No wonder the churches we belittle and look down on are the ones that are growing while ours are the ones that are stagnant or dying. These new churches embrace some main realities of our Christian faith, ones which make us so uncomfortable, we have all but discarded them because we are uncomfortable with the terms and the forms in which the experiences are expressed. The explanation simply has not been made that other terms could be used that would be more comfortable for our members.

Lately many of our congregations have adopted more upbeat worship styles, and some of them have found these changes may bring new people to their churches. I know of some churches that have started having Saturday evening "come as you are" services accompanied by brass, strings, drums, and more contemporary modes of music, which have proved more attractive to many people in our communities. But I know of other churches that have made much less notable changes, some that have added just a little upbeat flavor to their worship services, and some that have left their traditional morning worship intact but added another service with the contemporary elements, and they too have had better attendance at their services. We don't always have to make very radical changes in our churches in order to reclaim the fundamental realities of our faith we have lost touch with. A little goes a long way!

As it stands, in rejecting the salt of the new life and the fire of its power many of our churches are like restaurants that serve cold, unflavored food. The only clientele they can retain are those who frequent them out of habit, "for old-time's sake," or those who haven't discovered there are far better restaurants.

Another barrier to spreading the faith of Jesus is those churches who do not demonstrate the principle that underlies the new birth and new life in Christ, the principle of grace. Instead they live according to its opposing principle, the principle of law. People who participate in the lives of their churches without the motivation of interest, joy and meaning, those not empowered by the Spirit of the new life, do so out of a sense of habit and obligation. Many persist in this mode for decades. What a dull approach to worship and ministry they model when they could have been doing it all those years with great interest and enthusiasm.

Why wouldn't we want to make changes in our worship style that would not only attract new people to our churches but would also create an atmosphere that is more conducive to the basic experiences of Christian faith? There can be only one answer, selfishness. As difficult as it may be for us to admit, many of us who have spent our lives and ministries in such churches know that our people would rather have the kinds of worship and church life with which they are comfortable than to have those that include the fundamental experiences of Christian faith and effective evangelism. Woe unto a people who are so intent on maintaining what appeals to them that they reject what is true and effective.

I believe our basic appeal to those in our churches who resist these changes should be, "Try it, you'll like it." I know from experience that if many in our mainline churches would bend a little and allow themselves to experience what a difference some of these changes could make, they would begin to welcome them. If they could see their churches reaching new people and bringing healing to people's lives and families; if they could see a more involved and joyous spirit in their congregations, if they found that these experiences contributed to a closer relationship with our Lord for them and the other members of their churches, they would rejoice in what they saw and felt. The pleasure this would bring them should make the necessary modifications a lot easier. Jesus in fact did say, "My yoke is easy, and my burden is light" (Mt 11:30).

A genuine call for the renewal of the church involves a call to those of us who care to begin a concerted effort to pray for and take whatever action we can to convince the members of our congregations to humble themselves enough to give up their personal preferences and to adopt the priorities and methods that have proven effective in reaching people for our Lord. It is not enough to recommend such changes just because they have been found to "work." Not everything that "works" is right to do. These changes need to be made primarily because they are grounded in the primary principles of Christian faith and the biblical witness.

We would do well to encourage our people that if they will humble themselves to accept ways of worshiping and ministering with which they are not accustomed, our Lord will reward them to such an extraordinary degree they will be more than glad for having met the challenge. "Humble yourselves before the Lord, and he will exalt you" *(Jm 4:10)*.

8

Shepherds or Hired Hands?

The hired hand, who is not the shepherd and does not own the sheep, sees the wolf coming and leaves the sheep and runs away—and the wolf snatches them and scatters them (Jn 10:12).

The spinal column of all the church's work and accomplishments has been and still is the clergy, especially pastors of congregations. A United Methodist bishop has said, "What the pastor pushes moves." Pastors are an integral part of the life of the church, and obviously what they are or are not, what they do or do not do, *matters* for the church's life and ministry. For centuries Christian pastors were not only the shepherds of congregations, but they were almost the only educators and the only professional counselors. In many cases they were the community leaders to whom most people looked for guidance. Probably no profession has served the needs of people and the world nearly as much as have pastors.

In modern times there has developed throughout the church a "professionalism" that has infected an amazing number of pastors. They rarely express much interest in spiritual matters. Why would they? Their denominational superiors, credentialing boards, and committees very often seem more concerned about their educational degrees than they are about their spiritual standing. Too, there are many pastors (sadly enough, most of them in mainline denominational churches), who mirror the adverse spiritual conditions in the churches we have been describing in the preceding chapters. Their professional interests, their sermon topics, the language they use or avoid, and the impact they have on their congregations and communities (some quite admirable according to the world's terms) often is the kind that lacks "salt and fire." In fact pastors are largely responsible for the adverse conditions to which we have been referring.

It is of course a two-way street. The decline of the church's spiritual condition has influenced a similar decline among pastors and vice-versa. There is such a vicious cycle of spiritual illness that we would be hard put to identify its several causes, but to be sure the "hired hands" are near the core of what is the *matter* with the church.

The contrast Jesus drew between shepherds and hired hands strikes me as a scathing judgement against them. "The good shepherd lays down his life for the sheep.... The hired hand runs away because a hired hand does not care for the sheep. I am the good shepherd. I know my own and my own know me" *(Jn 10:11, 13-14)*.

If you have "eyes to see," a hired hand is relatively easy to spot. The passionate caring is not there. They are not the shepherds of our Lord's sheep; they are employees of the congregation. They are too little concerned to give the beloved sheep what they need. They are rather readers of the congregational "polls," carefully monitoring what the sheep want and giving that to them. They characteristically preach "positive" sermonettes that either make people feel good about themselves or not feel much at all, because their objective is to guard at all cost against upsetting the flock. The most professionally "successful" among them are skilled, self-serving politicians.

The "hired hands" of the church, "professionally" qualified though they may be, lack what the Pentecostal Christians call the "anointing." They do not reflect the profound and exciting New Life. They lack that spiritual unction, the "Spirit baptism," that is so obvious when it is there and when it is not. They too often are like teachers who have the same level of ignorance as their students. So far as what really *matters* in the Christian life, the realm of the spirit, they do not have much to offer their people.

I have observed several situations where such pastors were called on to perform a ministry that was very spiritual in nature. Not only were they obviously ill-prepared for the task, they actually seemed to be embarrassed about it. In the words of one of my seminary professors, who said about some seminary graduates, "They are like graduates of pilot's training who wear the pilot's uniform, carry the mystique of the pilot, talk in the pilot lingo, but cannot fly an airplane." This is perhaps a bit harsh, but it has an undeniable element of truth about such pastors.

One of the sad examples of this pastoral problem which is the current emphasis among the denominational clergy on "conflict resolution." Would that it was on biblical knowledge, impressive prophetic or pastoral preaching, or spiritual counsel. What a tragedy it is that a going clergy skill is an obviously secular professional role.

But the greatest danger is that this orientation and training might work too well. People in our churches could begin to assume their conflicts come from strong differences of opinion that can be resolved with the use of professional skill, when most of them stem from a lack of spiritual grounding on the part of one or both sides of the conflict. It is terrible to ignore a serious condition and try to persuade those involved in a conflict to practice "getting along," which of necessity is a superficial arrangement. It would be far better to view the conflict as unresolvable in human terms when it is a conflict between people of the New Life and people of the Old Life, as it so very often is.

The hired hand syndrome is marked by a phenomenal lack of courage on the part of pastors. Carlyle Marney, a great Southern Baptist prophet, used to say, "They haven't got the ego strength to say boo to a church mouse." When there is a gross giving way of discipleship to the Sunday morning "audience," as is the case in so many of our churches, too many pastors refuse to confront their congregations with this blatant "apostasy." We are so used to this pablum approach to the Gospel that any pastor who has the courage to challenge a congregation is immediately seen as harsh and untactful. Woe to a people who have allowed prophetic judgment to become unacceptable. As long as they cannot be judged, they cannot correct their misguided ways.

For many years I was unaware that this situation had deteriorated as badly as it has in some churches. The Gospel simply cannot be preached in them, for the congregation cannot tolerate hearing the Gospel. The Good News is not good to everyone who hears it. When people chronically resist the Gospel, the Good News becomes bad news because to hear the Gospel is to experience spiritual judgment. Although he did not come to judge the world, Jesus said anyone who rejects him has by that rejection invoked serious judgment.

> "I do not judge anyone who hears my words and does not keep them, for I came not to judge the world, but to save the world. The one who rejects me and does not receive my word has a judge; on the last day the word that I have spoken will serve as judge (Jn 12:47-48).

9

First Things First

Ninety percent of all we do in the church has absolutely nothing to do with the Gospel! (Bishop Handy Hancock, United Methodist, retired).

One of the greatest contributions the church has made has been to teach and influence individuals, communities, and even nations and cultures about better ordering of the priorities of their lives. The experience of "salvation" itself can be seen as a basic ordering of priorities. It establishes the spiritual life as the highest priority. Doing that tends to put other priorities into right order. "But strive first for the kingdom of God and his righteousness, and all these things will be given to you as well" *(Mt 6:33)*.

It is axiomatic that those who are not working on something important will either be working on something unimportant, or they will be doing nothing. Church folk, both staff and laity, being members of a public institution, have to do something. If we do not work on evangelism, the empowerment of our members, missional efforts in our communities, or the healing of broken lives and families, what will we do? Too often we can be seen doing exactly what my dear friend, Bishop Handy Hancock, claims in the quote above. When we look at the situation honestly, it is hard to dispute that assertion. Very little of what we do is dedicated to gospel endeavors.

If we consider seriously how much time we spend on genuine ministry, the "apostasy" of the contemporary church looms large before us. Charles Allen, a famous Methodist preacher in Atlanta and Houston, once said, "If we spent one-tenth of the time actually going out and talking to people about Jesus Christ than we spend in meetings about it, we would have converted the world long ago."

Most of our members seldom realize this mis-ordering of our priorities, because the focus of attention is usually on lesser *matters*: our facilities, our equipment and decor, our finances, our meals, our meetings, and our programs that range from exercise sessions to book clubs. There's nothing wrong with any of these, but they are not nearly as important as the things we should be doing. In order to get our priorities corrected we would probably have to close down most of these programs and meetings altogether to allow the vacuum of real ministry to become clear to our people.

Another form of this problem is our absurd expansion of what ministry is. In the absence of real ministry, probably because we could not tolerate the realization that we are doing very little of it, we have broadened our definition of ministry to include everything from paying for the altar flowers to greeting people with a smile. Jesus and his early followers would be saddened by such a trivial view of his ministry. Of course there's nothing wrong with any of these activities either; it is just that we should reserve the word "ministry" for the missional efforts for which the church was called into being.

Not only is spiritual ministry being neglected, but ministries to physical human needs right in the communities where our churches are located are being slighted. From the time Jesus told his followers to care for the poor and preach the gospel to the poor up until the present, the church has addressed the problems of the poor in myriad ways and places. Yet too many of our contemporary congregations simply ignore the needs of the poor altogether.

The church I served in Connecticut exemplified all the "apostate" characteristics mentioned so far in these pages. Amazingly it was involved in virtually no ministry at all, yet its most obvious departure from what the Christian church is supposed to be was that it had no real relationship with the people in its neighborhood. Several years ago the church spent more than $400,000 on repairs of the church's bell tower yet the neighborhood around it displays all the problems of poverty. The congregation does virtually nothing to assist the people who live nearby, yet they take great pride in themselves because they serve two meals a month to the poor. No wonder this church is dying. God has no need for it.

Our recruitment efforts are also marked by our ill-chosen priorities. We expend a great deal of time and effort recruiting people for responsibilities and tasks that are comparatively uninspiring when they could be challenged to take on important and meaningful ministries. How long has it been since you heard a pastor ask for volunteers in the church who would meet and plan ways to go out into their community and find people who would be responsive to the Gospel? It would probably surprise us to find there are people in most of our churches who have been waiting for such an opportunity but no one has ever organized one.

One frustrated layperson told me how a call to serve our Lord had been gnawing at him for months. He said he was so moved by the challenge he had felt for serving the Lord in so many significant ways that he thought when he offered himself to his church he would be asked to go to some foreign country, or at least to reach out to the unchurched or needy in his community. One Sunday morning during worship service he went down the aisle to affirm his willingness to serve the Lord. Several weeks later, sure enough, he was called by one of the lay leaders of his church and asked to serve, but it was not the kind of assignment he expected. He was asked to help take up the offering.

Every year in every church I have served when the nominating committee met to come up with people who could be elected to fill the various positions in the organization, I have wondered what would happen if we asked some people to do some really demanding work for their church's ministry. I truly believe some of our folks would answer such a call with great enthusiasm.

How differently would our people respond to the church's financial campaigns if we offered them the opportunity to contribute to some more inspiring ministries than are usually included in our annual budgets? What if they saw listed in the budget such items as a study center staffed with capable teachers for elementary and high school students who were having trouble in school, a program where folk could render help to families who have behavior difficulties with their children, or a center staffed for assisting the particular needs of single-parent families? There are any number of worthwhile ministry possibilities that would motivate increased financial support from church members.

One of the main reasons I believe we do not attract more people to our churches to be involved in ministries is that few of them are genuinely challenging or have anything to do with the basic work to which the church is called. We do not give them the opportunities to serve in any significant way, so why should they bother? The effort to get our churches to put first things first must be on the agenda of any call for the renewal of the church.

10

Education Without Learning

Knowledge is power (Francis Bacon)

After the fall of the Roman Empire, with few exceptions, formal education as we know it had its beginnings in the Western Christian church, and most of those were established to train the clergy. The church later started schools for children and lay adults. This pattern continued in the American colonies with the first schools on the new continent being brought into being by the need to educate clerics, with the two leading universities, Harvard and Yale, established to educate the Congregational clergy. Later the church in America began numerous schools for children plus colleges and universities for adults.

On countless foreign mission fields, especially in Third World countries, the Christian church has introduced educational programs for people who otherwise would never have had such an opportunity. To its eternal credit, the church has been the pioneer of education in the world.

To this day there are a multitude of church-related colleges and universities in the U.S. The faculties and administrations of many of them, to preserve academic freedom, have altered their relationships with their founding churches so they are not nearly as close as they once were. Others have broken off the relationship altogether, but this is no fault of the church. Given the nature and values of higher education in our time, it was more or less a necessary development. In many cases there has been such a sensitivity on the part of church people and their leaders that they have actually advocated changes in the relationship between the church and educational institutions rather than resisting them.

Nearly every church in the U.S. has a Sunday school and most of them have a Bible-study program of some kind. Not until the early 20th century did the concept of a Christian education program begin to take form. A staff position of a Christian education director also was established in larger local congregations with special seminary programs introduced for formal Christian education training. The ecumenical Christian Education Association was organized in 1903. Except for the worship services, these educational programs, with lay or professional staffing, are no doubt one of the most abiding ministries in Christian churches.

With all this commitment of human and financial resources, one would think our educational programs in local churches would be of a fairly high quality. However, this is anything but the case. There is probably no educational program anywhere in which the students learn less than do the participants in most of the educational programs of local churches. You can ask the most basic questions about the Scriptures, for instance, and adults who have been attending Sunday school for decades do not know the answers. Even with such basic questions like, "What are the four Gospels?" you can get nothing but blank stares. Why is this the case?

Exceptions exist to be sure, and they are to be highly commended for reaching higher than the existing standards, but most of the educational programs in our local churches do not teach people much at all, because we require and expect so little study on the part of the students. In fact to call them students is a misnomer. We do not have student bodies. Just as in our church membership in general, the young people are just audiences. They attend but actually learn only a modicum of new knowledge. Hardly anyone is challenged. Little is required of them. If an assignment is involved in the program or series, not many of the class members or the teacher take it very seriously. We give no examinations and we almost never use measuring instruments of any kind. We actually do not expect our class members to learn much.

Most of the local church's educational programs are put together on a "What would they be interested in?" basis.

The place to start is in the adoption of purposes, goals and objectives for the education program. It would be unnecessary for each local church to work at this. Different curricula with varied purposes could be developed by the central denominational education departments. To some extent this is already being done, but we usually have to get materials for a program before we find out the objectives they seek to reach with the class members. What would seem far better would be for the brochures and catalogues to identify the different programs by the purposes of each one instead of by catchy titles. The ideal approach would be for a class and its teacher along with the pastor or appropriate staff person to clarify some specific educational need that particular group has and then seek the material that would best meet that need. With all the resources and talent and well informed people that are available to our churches, that should not be a difficult task, and it would be a very creative, interesting, and rewarding one.

It is little wonder that there is no coherent body of Christian spiritual, biblical, theological, ethical and moral knowledge shared by our church members. How could we expect them to talk about their faith in an informed way to unchurched people when we do not make any serious effort to make them knowledgeable about it. Why are we surprised when church attendance is substituted for Christian discipleship when our people have not been educated as to what discipleship in our contemporary world entails? It is not surprising there are so many adverse comments made by people in our congregations against their pastors' preaching and teaching when we have made no real effort to impress upon them in any intentional, system-

What's the Matter with the Church?

atic and documented way the profound depths and scope of the Christian faith.

Yet if you suggest a more challenging approach to education to any pastor or Christian education director, you will most likely get answers like, "Yes, that would be far better, but not many would attend such a class." So we substitute attendance numbers for learning. We are like the man who started an auto mechanic training school and found he could attract many students to his school and make a great deal of money by making the training very enjoyable and undemanding and charging an expensive fee for it.

But he told his wife, "For pity sake, don't take our car to any of these guys."

Offering undemanding classes in order to attract more people obviously does not produce any educational gain. If we offered more challenging educational programs, we might produce fewer deeply committed Christian witnesses; but as it is now, we are producing virtually none.

This was not always the case. Two unfortunate developments in the history of church education brought us to our current dilemma. Sunday schools first began in Great Britain and America in the beginning years of the industrial revolution before public education made schools available for poor children. Started by churches in the neighborhoods where the factories were located, these church schools aimed to teach children to read and write. Scriptures were the most convenient literature for the teachers to use. Thus the Sunday school became a major evangelism arm of the church, a comfortable door by which people who were won to the Christian faith could enter the life of churches in their communities. The positive impact of these programs on the quality of life in these communities was immeasurable.

So these church-based educational programs conveyed real knowledge to people where ignorance formerly prevailed, and unchurched people could be invited to Sunday school where they were more comfortable than they would be in worship services. Gradually public schools assumed the major responsibility for children's education;

many children of unchurched families no longer came to church to learn to read and write, and therefore not nearly as many were taught the Scriptures. When these children became adults and graduates of public schools, they had no longer been exposed to basic scriptural knowledge.

Rather than develop along solid educational and evangelical lines, classes in our churches tend basically to be sessions from which fragments of concrete Biblical and theological knowledge might hopefully "stick" in the minds of the attendees. So the evangelical value of Sunday schools has been almost entirely lost. Some classes have long since become a kind of "graduate school" for church members with people recruited from worship services to take this "advanced" step in churchness.

Christian education could give both evangelism and church growth a significant boost were we to raise the consciousness of class members so they would regard the church school program as a more informal, personable, and comfortable environment to which they could invite their unchurched friends, family members, and acquaintances for a true learning experience.

This could be a huge task, yet if we would commit regularly to make a substantial change in our churches' educational programs, we could see wonderful things happen in our churches. Just think how it would be if a number of church members were called to make concerted, efforts to bring solid learning to such programs in our churches.

If Francis Bacon was right and "knowledge is power," it can be safely said that ignorance is weakness. Bacon's statement has certainly proven more obvious as knowledge and technology has advanced in exponential proportions in the post modern world. Education certainly *matters*. The renewal of the church in our time depends in large measure on its ability to produce informed students.

"Happy are those who find wisdom, and those who get understanding, for her income is better than the silver, and her revenue better than gold. She is more precious than jewels, and nothing you desire can compare with her" *(Pr 3:13-15).*

11

Not like Us

There is no longer Jew or Greek, there is no longer slave or free, there is no longer male and female; for all of you are one in Christ Jesus (Gal 3:28).

When we look at the issues that make up the content of the church's life and work and ask which of them really *matter*, diversity certainly qualifies as a real priority. Historically the church has brought all kinds and classes of people together. It was born in a class society with class-structured cultures. Often it was virtually the only fellowship that brought the classes together. There were a number of cases in places like Rome, for instance, where wealthy families hosted worship and fellowship for their fellow Christians, many of whom were poor.

Jesus obviously emphasized diversity when he selected his original twelve disciples. They represented disparate strata of their society. Most of the people who followed Jesus were obviously poor, but it is clear that he had some wealthy people among his followers. Joseph of Arimathea, for instance, whom all three synoptic gospels report as having given the burial place for Jesus' body, was a wealthy and renowned citizen. It seems there were people from all social and economic levels who were Christ's followers. Today mainline Protestant communions have mostly developed into organizations of fairly affluent people. Except for those churches in poor neighborhoods whose congregations are largely made up of the local folk, the poor and minorities are under represented in their memberships.

This situation developed as churches sprang up in the burgeoning suburbs of the U.S., so the centrally located city churches were no longer attended by residents in their neighborhoods. For inner-city churches as the members moved or died, the dwindling congregations were made up of "hangers on" who were uncomfortable rubbing shoulders with those of other races or from a lower class.

Usually the discomfort went both ways so that the members did not feel like inviting the poor people who had disrupted their old neighborhoods into their congregations of which they had such vivid memories of being prestigious churches. The old guard church members were able to tolerate a few poor people who were appropriately grateful for their generosity and their being undiscriminating, but if the number of poor people began to increase appreciably, souls became quite insecure.

The poorer people willing to be part of this scene tend to be few and far between anyway. They are barely tolerated and treated by most with a cool paternalism. They are seldom treated as genuine peers. This is a subtle problem, and most church people in the midst of these sociological changes have no clue about the underlying issues involved. Most of them justify their behavior and attitudes, if they are at all aware of them, and do not believe there is anything wrong with them.

Such class divides are so much a part of the church in our time that three decades ago the first literature of the Church Growth Institute in California cited one of the characteristics of growing churches as increasing in homogenous units, attracting people who are generally like the existing members, and advocated that churches make it the main principle of their church growth efforts. The Institute could perceive nothing wrong with this principle, and few voiced criticism of their message, although I did hear Bishop Marion Edwards, to his immense credit, complain that while he admired the work of the Institute, he had a problem with its sociological view, for he thought it justified the lack of diversity in our churches by proposing just the opposite as a method for church growth.

This attitude of exclusiveness among church members and pastors who often have refused to confront and condemn it can only be regarded as blatantly unchristian. People who view the poor and minorities this way have obviously not experienced the conversion in their thinking that makes them welcome all God's people into their fellowships as members of one Body in Christ. All people, the poor and the rich, minority or not, are to be seen as potential members of his Body. They are all to be graciously accepted into the family of Christ. Anything short of that is a violation of his "new commandment" to love one another as he has loved us.

There is a popular rationalization that seeks to spiritualize Jesus' strong emphasis and insistence that his followers preach the gospel to the poor. Many times I have heard it explained that Jesus was not referring to material poverty. But it seems pretty obvious that Jesus was not speaking symbolically about the poor, but was interacting with them and commending some of them as models of what pleases God. There is no way to escape the interpretation that Christ was talking about people in financial poverty, and anyone who has dealt with all classes of people can see why he stressed this so much. The poor usually need more help than people who are wealthy or solvent.

In the first place, poor people are far more apt to be responsive to the Gospel because they do not have all the crutches they can depend on as do people who have more resources. Our evangelism efforts need to remain cognizant of the fact that in general people who suffer from significant pain and adversity are far more apt to receive the saving grace and lordship of Christ than people who are reasonably comfortable. And if we are interested in the Gospel influencing our society toward a more moral and humane environment and are at all sincere about wanting "the kingdom of God to come on earth," we must seek in every way possible to see that the Gospel is preached to the poor.

In every city and town, crime and inhumane and uncaring conditions prevail in the communities where people are poor. This is where our churches cannot minimize their efforts at evangelism because this is where it is most needed. People facing crises in their lives tend to be desperate to find succor and solutions for their problems. The poor have always been more prone to feel the need for the Lord in their lives and therefore are more likely to hear and receive his Good News. Nothing is more vital, essential or rightful for the church community than loving their neighbors, whom Jesus defined as those with a need to which we can minister. At the same time, nothing is more in need of renewal than the unloving attitudes of church people toward their poor neighbors.

Let us work and pray toward the end that the church of our Lord will be open and welcoming to people of all classes and races, colors, languages and ethnic backgrounds.

The first Pentecost took place when the Christians gathered in Jerusalem that day were of such an ethnically, culturally, and racially diverse crowd of worshipers that they scarcely had a common language except for the language of the Spirit. "Parthians, Medes, Elamites, and residents of Mesopotamia, Judea and Cappadocia, Pontus and Asia, Phrygia and Pamphylia, Egypt and the parts of Libya belonging to Cyrene, and visitors from Rome, both Jews and proselytes, Cretans and Arabs – in our own languages we hear them speaking about God's deeds of power" (Ac 2:9-11).

Surely, if we are really interested in a powerful move of the Holy Spirit and renewal in our churches, we will seek maximum diversity in our congregations as something that really *matters*.

12

The Little Foxes

Catch us the foxes, the little foxes, that ruin the vineyards – for our vineyards are in blossom (Song 2:15).

Throughout its history the church has brought into its service a multitude of "heavyweights," and it has made myriads of great Christian disciples of the ordinary and even the less than ordinary. I heard Carlyle Marney, the late Southern Baptist scholar and pulpit giant, once say that if you go to any town and find out who the community leaders are and those who are most respected by their neighbors, you will find that most of them are active members of churches.

This has certainly proven to be true – with few exceptions – in my experience. One of the greatest contributions the church has made is that of changing people for the better and giving them an opportunity to use their gifts and talents in the service of utmost value. The numbers of these people, should they be compiled in one list, would be staggering.

But there have always been the "little foxes that spoil the vine," those who spoil the climate of the congregation with petty and negative behavior. It only takes one of these to wreck the joy in any church gathering. Gifted leaders in the past could often mitigate the destructive efforts of the "little foxes" because there were larger congregations to draw on, but this has changed in the past few decades because with the declining membership where is harder to drown out the strident voices. With fewer church members to draw on, there aren't as many gifted leaders and opinion makers as before so the church loses its prestige and effectiveness in communities and "heavyweights" have less motivation to become involved in its life and work.

Too, in the small and declining churches the little foxes have more say in the life of the church so now you often find the church left to the leadership of those with small and petty attitudes, further weakening the church because those in charge lack ability, imagination, character and courage to be a significant presence in the neighborhood.

In my effort to learn as much as I could about the measures that had proved effective for church growth, I have come to see the little foxes as the "enemies of Christ." This might seem harsh, especially in the light of our long history of never confronting people about their sins and weaknesses. Our chronic commitment to tact and diplomacy allows nay-sayers to take over. We deal with them under the false assumption that they are just troublesome Christians, but they are much worse. Let us not forget that the people the apostle Paul considered to be "enemies of the cross of Christ" were church members of his day.

"Brothers and sisters, join in imitating me, and observe those who live according to the example you have in us. For many live as enemies of the cross of Christ; I have often told you of them, and now I tell you even with tears" *(Ph. 3:17-18)*. The people Paul dubbed "enemies of the cross of Christ" did not identify themselves as such. They did not go around saying, "We are the enemies of the cross of Christ." They would have been highly insulted to hear this because they thought of themselves as good Christians, but they sought to counter genuine Christian doctrine and opposed the progress of the church and its mission. This is precisely what negative detractors in our churches do and how they think about themselves, certainly not as enemies of the cross. Yet they oppose the ways and means to best reach people with the message that God loves them enough to die for them.

They pose formidable barriers to the legitimate ministries of the church because they usually lack a personal experience and a personal relationship with Christ (although they have no idea this is true) and the indwelling of the Holy Spirit which is actually something entirely foreign to them. What they lack most of all is the "salt" and the "fire."

These little foxes are usually devotees of civil religion and worship a god of comfort and convenience, one who does not require much at all of them. They prefer the deity of the Sunday "audience," the god of the bylaws and constitution of the church, instead of the God of the Scriptures, and the God of Jesus Christ. I am not advocating we treat the little foxes with meanness and uncaring, but rather we should know what they are and not credit them as Christians in good standing. We should deal with them as kindly as possible, standing firmly against their efforts to frustrate the will of God for the church.

The little foxes can arouse such opposition to their church leaders as too seriously prevent them from being effective. Many a pastorate has failed because of their efforts. Too few members of our churches are willing to stand with those attacked and oppose the detractors in such "lynchings." The cowardice of denominational staff people who tend to be more interested in job security than in truth makes them resist taking any positions against the little foxes. Too often they are willing to sacrifice the pastor who is under attack by these people in order to avoid being the next in line.

If we are to bring renewal to the Christian church, we must aggressively counteract the efforts and influence of the little foxes. Let's not be so "kind" that we are not willing to contend vigorously against these "enemies of the cross of Christ." Christ warned us that we are not only to be as "innocent as doves" but also "wise as serpents" (Mt 10:16).

If we want to see the renewal of the church, we will have to pray for the conversion of these people and for the power to overcome them. We must, lovingly of course, stand against the destructive efforts of the little foxes wherever and whenever we see them.

What's the Matter with the Church?

13

Keeping it in the Family

"Looking back, I think that church was a shame–based on my family" (Melanie Beattie).

The Christian church originated and continued in its early years with an attitude of openness regarding its internal problems and outside accusations. It is difficult to determine how long this attitude between church leaders and members prevailed, because church historians have not seen this as an issue of interest for their research. But it is probable that openness began to wither away early in the church's history. There is a tendency in all of us to try to prevent adverse information about us, about our family, about our business, about our agency, and about our church from becoming public knowledge. And so it is today that a church suffers when there is a rigid commitment among its members to this stance.

Somewhere along the way the members of churches have come to perceive their fellowships as closed societies. Too often they believe their problems are no one's business but theirs. We are prone to think of our church as a private and "sacred" family, making us all the more protective of letting the public view its flaws.

We may find it difficult to understand why Catholic bishops have kept trying to sweep under the carpet the child molestation by many priests, but most likely this attitude of keeping it within the sacred family played a significant role in it. This defensiveness caused the bishops to lose sight of sound logic. If they had immediately referred the priests who were charged with these offenses to the authorities, the sinful behavior would not have contributed to such a bad witness for the church. On the contrary, prompt corrective action probably would have heightened rather than lowered the confidence most of their own parishioners and the general public had in the church.

Representatives of the media, who seek information about problems that have arisen in a local congregation, are seen as intruders. Reporters who inquire about such *matters* are often met with a cool non-responsiveness and at times, outright hostility. There is a widespread adverse view of the press among Americans, so the ideas of the church as a sacred family, and the popular distrust of the media in this country, have combined to create a strong defensive attitude on the part of church members when it comes to publicity about controversial issues and developments that have arisen in their congregations.

I have found this attitude toward the press is usually strongest among church people who have the most to hide. A reporter from a local paper in a New England city where I served a pastorate interviewed me and several church members from both sides of a conflict that was brewing in that congregation – essentially about the opposition some members took to positions I was advocating on social issues and ways to foster growth in the church.

The reporter wrote what I thought was a fair article about the conflict, but the newspaper received several letters objecting to the "intrusion" into the church's private affairs. I soon realized these complaints came from people opposed to my ministry, but who also had the most to hide. They had stooped to blatant slander and racism to arouse people against me and my wife. I have learned that this kind of reaction to the press is usually not found among

What's the Matter with the Church?

gracious and positive-minded folk in our churches.

In ancient times those who chose the canon of both the Hebrew and Christian Scriptures did not hold only favorable attitudes about the people of their respective traditions and congregations. That is why Scripture is replete with sordid stories about the failings of the people of God, the adultery and murder by David, Saul's insanity, the many instances of disobedience to God on the part of the people, and on and on into the Christian Scriptures which refer to weakness, cowardice, betrayal, and very serious problems in the burgeoning Christian congregations. Paul even wrote about the adultery of a man with his stepmother in the Corinthian congregation and advocated his excommunication from the church (1 Co. 5:1) (To his credit, however, Paul also advocated the reaffirming love for and the reinstatement of this member in the fellowship when he had repented of wrong behavior (2 Co. 2:5-11). Paul most probably did not intend his remarks to become public, but the canonizers of the New Testament certainly did. So the entire Scriptures did not shirk from portraying the people of God, "warts and all."

The church I have referred to that I served in New England had virtually all the failings I have noted: the lack of "salt" and "fire," the poverty of the "baptism" of Jesus, and a good many "little foxes." But in reflection I must sadly admit that I, too, contributed to the situation for as pastor I had ceased to be a shepherd. I became angry, stopped caring about the people and was more interested in prevailing in the conflict than in helping the congregation solve its problems. In fact, looking back, it has been painful to realize I was the main cause of the problems. Many of the criticisms were petty and mean, many of the accusations against me were patently false, but I am convinced they would never have been made had I been the shepherd I should have been.

But whoever the main cause of the controversy was in that case, the attitude of secrecy had the appearance of having very deep roots in that congregation. And it deserves our attention if we want to see renewal in our churches because it has a crippling effect in congregation much in the same way that it has dysfunctional families. It is more than just a defensive stance. It is, in fact, socio-pathological. Most mental healthcare professions today acknowledge this trait as being a central symptom or cause in dysfunctional families. When problems exist in the family like substance abuse, alcoholism, physical or sexual abuse, there is characteristically an effort by the family members to keep these *matters* inside the family circle.

Congregations that routinely experience internal conflict have all the traits of a dysfunctional family. A pastor of a neighboring church in New England went through a similar situation to mine at the time of my ordeal, and was fired by his church. I readily related to his description of his pastorate as an "abusive" relationship. And because I was being subjected to the most vicious, slanderous and false accusations by some of the officers of the church I was serving, I had begun to strenuously steel my soul against a constant pummeling of attacks and insults.

Another nearby pastor said, "I don't believe these accusations because nobody could be that bad!" When the regional conference minister spoke to the press about what had happened at the church, he said it was a problem of "style," which struck me as absurd, evasive, offensive and dishonest under the circumstances. I have encountered all too few denominational staff people who are actually gifted people, and I have often wondered if that is why some of them are uncaring and dishonest at times. One who is not very professionally talented might have far greater tendencies to lack concern for a person who is victimized by others and to use dishonesty to keep himself or herself in a favorable light.

Sunshine laws that began to be put on the books for government and public agencies in the 1950s and '60s emerged from the realization it is much healthier for any organization to have the light of public observation to be shown on their deliberations. Unfortunately too many church members and denominational staff people have not entertained the idea that openness is healthy and that secretiveness is unhealthy.

The notion of the church as a closed, sacred family does not appear to grow out of a genuine, religious response. It smacks much more of superstition, for it has been universally recognized that the Christian faith encourages openness and security. Surely a fellowship that trusts God for its security should not be concerned about the public knowing the truth about its internal affairs. We may not want people in our communities to be reminded that church folk have human weaknesses, but the general public cannot be ignorant of this fact.

Our time-honored American constitutional principle regarding the freedom of the press which church people so often seek to restrict and diminish is a tradition that has been highly honored and revered in our country from its earliest days. No one can doubt but that this has been enormously instrumental in bringing corruption in government and criminal activities in business to the notice of the public. The role of the media in protecting against unethical and illegal activity in our society is far more "sacred" than the privacy of our church affairs.

This "keep it in the family" syndrome has adversely impacted our evangelism at the gravest level. To get people who are unchurched to see church folk as people with whom they can relate, we should let it be known that members of Christian congregations are in fact sinners who have the same problems and moral lapses as those who are unchurched. We need to have the church understood by the outside world as made up of fallible and sinful human beings who know what they are and admit it. One of the most serious evangelism problems the church has is that a large majority of unchurched people view too many church members as either too "saintly" for them to associate with, or as hypocritical snobs who think themselves too good to associate with "sinners."

The opening up of congregational and denominational activity to the public so that a healthy light can shine in on their troubles can enable them to foster the honest image that their people are susceptible to the same failings as people who are not active in the life of a church. Openness should be an indispensable item on our renewal agenda. Surely the God of the Christian faith would not want to be seen by those outside the church as having forged a closed and secret society.

God does not appear to be overly concerned about the bad example some people set. An all-powerful God can keep any adverse witness under raps if God wants to. Perhaps our God finds these "bad examples" of valuable use since those people who are worried that they are not "good" enough to please God can see that they belong with these struggling Christians. And in this connection we can explain to them that God wants people to come as they are. In fact, they cannot come into a personal relationship with God unless they sincerely admit their wrongs. After all, if nothing is wrong with us before we seek a relationship with God, we would not need God's forgiveness, which is what the Gospel of grace is all about.

"Please, Lord, help us to open the windows of public view to our congregations in order that we might become a people more like you. We know you as a God of humility, honesty and openness. Unless we understand that you empower us for the task you have given us only if we make clear who and how you really are to those who do not know you, we will surely fail in accomplishing it. Amen."

14

Unopened Gifts

Now we have received not the spirit of the world, but the Spirit that is from God, so that we may understand the gifts bestowed on us by God (1 Co 2:12).

Surely no one would argue against the idea that the phenomenal achievements of the church in the world have been accomplished through the efforts of Christian disciples whose gifts have been given to them and activated by the "salt" and the "fire." The church has amassed an incredible array of human talents, given and guided by the Holy Spirit, to plan and implement the Spirit's ministries. No other organization in human history has accomplished anything like the church's recruitment and deployment of human gifts and abilities.

But the widespread infestation of what has been called "civil religion" has resulted in Christian discipleship being replaced by a comfortable "spirituality." Even though people of the "salt and fire" are empowered with spiritual gifts for the innumerable tasks of Christian ministry, often congregations who are overly influenced by civil religion want nothing to do with this kind of discipleship. Their purpose is clearly contra-distinctive to that of the movement begun by Jesus because they are uninterested in spreading the redeeming love of God to as many people as possible; they would rather provide for their congregations a very comfortable spiritual support organization. The spiritual gifts of the devotees of civil religion are therefore virtually untapped and unempowered by the Holy Spirit. They are left dormant never to be realized unless true Christian conversion comes to them.

Who would leave Christmas gifts sitting around unopened long after the holidays? This is what happens in so many of our churches as the multitude of very special, colorful spiritual gifts, *de colores*, sit around our congregations unopened. Taken together they amount to a vast storehouse of untapped, human and spiritual resources. To have these packages opened and the gifts in them marshaled for the service of the church's mission is a crying need to which any serious effort of church renewal must address itself. Surely there has never been a comparable waste of human resources.

In most of our churches little attention is paid to the New Testament concept of ministry gifts. Too often we give the various forms of service in the church to whoever will take them so there is little relationship between people's gifts and the roles they are elected to serve. Is it any wonder that our ministries suffer a lack of effectiveness? We hardly ever know what gifts most of our members have been given, because most mainline churches exert little effort to discover them. So frequently we select people to responsibilities for which they are ill-equipped.

If talented ballerinas are assigned the responsibilities of stage hands, both the dancing and the props will be notably inferior. So why should we expect something different in the church? This mismatching produces a wholesale loss of interest and a high degree of apathy. There are no ways to provide even partial solutions to this problem unless we see a multitude of admirers of Jesus become his disciples. First there must be the "salt" before the gifts can even be perceived; then there must be the "fire" before they can be empowered to function effectively. The task of church renewal must begin with an effort to influence the leaders of the church towards a genuine experience of conversion from admirers to disciples.

Beyond the need for more of the "fruits" of salt and fire in our congregations, a major overhauling of the prevailing understanding of the responsibilities of a pastor is also needed. Little effort is normally given to identify our pastors' ministry gifts so that their congregations' expectations of their ministry would be consonant with those gifts. With few exceptions, this just is not the way we do it. Instead of considering the spiritual gifts of a candidate for a position as a pastor, we arbitrarily assign to the whole package of responsibilities traditionally assigned to our pastors.

We expect all pastors to take on the same set of responsibilities we have assigned to all former pastors. The problem is that there are few pastors who have all the gifts needed. Some pastors cover the expected responsibilities better than others, but no single minister can discharge all of them effectively. The pastorate as it is now is almost universally understood is an impossible role for any human being.

Some of these responsibilities could be assigned to members of the congregation who are more gifted in administrative tasks. This would lighten the pastor's role to a more realistic degree so they could maximize their strengths for the church's ministry. As we said, church members would serve in capacities to which their gifts fit them, and this would mean that more people would be involved in the work of the church in constructive ways, which in itself always brings more life to a congregation.

People who have not received the "salt" cannot perceive the right work they should be doing, so not only are many of the efforts of our church people made without adequate spiritual power, the work that is done in many instances is also the wrong work. Those who feel they should be doing something for the church, but lack spiritual insight to perceive the work that is right, set about doing a host of mundane things that do not extend the Gospel to people nor spiritually build up our members. This is why we hear countless times, "Much of the work of the church is just busy work"

Deprived of the ministry gifts of all its members, a congregation may settle for a kind of mediocrity. Challenges for the church like the Great Commission are largely ignored. How much that is done by pastors and church members can we honestly say is meaningfully related to this great passage? "Go therefore and make disciples of all nations, baptizing them in the name of the Father and of the Son and of the Holy Spirit, and teaching them to obey everything I have commanded you. And remember, I am with you always, to the end of the age" *(Mt 28:19-20)*.

United Methodist Bishop Emerson Colaw has admitted with bold honesty that this commission is "rarely addressed" and that church leaders dismiss it by saying, "God has called us to be faithful, not successful." This, Bishop Colaw asserts, commits us to "dying faithfully."

Without exaggeration I honestly think this is the greatest misfortune in human history. It strikes me that for the greatest institution in history, the only one to actually become global, the only one to amass such an incredible number and variety of ministries to people, the one to change more people's lives than all the other institutions put together, to take on in so many quarters such a bland mediocrity is history's unrivaled tragedy.

This, to be sure, is a *matter* that *matters* for the renewal of the church as much as any. It is somehow too easy for us to ignore the Great Commission, but no issue deserves our attention more than this one.

"Dear Lord, We offer ourselves as your instruments for you to channel the power of your Spirit for a revival of excellence among the people everywhere who are called by your name. Amen."

15

Dying for a Good Cause

Because, in truth, because they have misled my people, saying, "Peace," when there is no peace; and because, when the people build a wall, these prophets smear whitewash on it that it. Say to those who smear whitewash on it that it shall fall (Ez 13:10-11a).

For many years the denominational staffs, boards, and committees have been the avenues to ordination. These groups have also deployed a great number of people throughout the world to preach the Gospel, to provide educational programs and institutions, to establish and build churches, and assist indigenous people with healthcare and disease prevention, engineering, building and farming. Such an enormous deployment can hardly be exaggerated.

The various denominations serve a real need by providing an array of choices of doctrines, theology, government, worship, and style. When there was only one choice it was inevitable that alternatives would be created, because it is obviously not possible to establish a church with which all Christians are satisfied. However many have been established at any given time, more have always been needed to serve people whose beliefs and preferences were not found in the existing ones. It must be granted that in many senses the diverse denominations are "good news," while they are also the institutional bad news of the divided Body of Christ.

It has been the conflict among individual beliefs and preferences that has led to the creation of a variety of denominations. These strongholds of conflicting doctrines and polity are most formidable barriers to Christian unity. When Luther first led Protestants away from the Catholic church, it might have been far better had alternative congregations been allowed to form under a more tolerant and flexible church. Obviously that was impossible then because the doctrinal and liturgical rigidity of the Catholic church prevented such congregations from being formed under its auspices.

With the evolving direction of the Catholic church in our time it seemed for a while that we might be moving toward that possibility, but this no longer appears likely. Any attempt at real, organic union, even among the Protestants, faces the turf protectiveness of the denominations. So, for instance, the efforts of the Consultation On Church Union (COCU) have slowed down to a crawl. Getting different denominations just to work together is difficult enough; getting them to unite organically is virtually impossible at any time in the foreseeable future.

Even though it was largely unyielding attitudes on both sides that initially sparked the formation of the Protestant communions, now it is mainly unyielding turf consciousness and uncompromising doctrinal, liturgical, and organizational forms that drive the refusal of the denominations to enter into organizational unity with one another. Many of the individual members of our congregations would like to see a melding together of the Body of Christ under one aegis, but the denominational leaders are too protective of their jobs and property to provide substantial leadership toward church union.

As far as doctrinal, liturgical, and organizational differences are concerned, I don't think such unions would necessarily require as much compromise as we might think. If all parties of the union could simply grant to the others the freedom to retain the essential aspects of their tradition, they could function under the same denominational roof. But issues more basic to the church's original mission need to become parts of denominational life and work.

Many denominational staff people appear to have even less "salt" and "fire" than our local churches. They are basically polished and professional composites of the wrong thinking and behavior we can find prevalent in local congregations.

Again, it is partly due I'm sure to my personal preferences, but I do not believe this problem is nearly as serious in the United Methodist church as it is in other denominations because of the superintendency level of the Methodist clergy. Instead of pastors reporting to a central executive and staff of a conference or presbytery, they report to a district superintendent who is normally a one-person staff with clerical support who has been appointed from a pastorate to supervise a district of pastors and churches. And they are returned to a pastorate when they are appointed again. The superintendents are therefore just one step removed from the pastors they supervise, and they actually function as a pastor to pastors and not just in name only as is the case with most other denominations. The Methodists have no permanent centralized bureaucracy.

As professional administrators most denominational staff positions tend to be closed to people of the salt and fire. Those with personal gifts of ministry empowered by the Christ's "baptism" tend not to fit into such "teams," so this leaves us with too many denominational staff members who lack effectiveness in enabling and enhancing the church's main missions. Candidates for staff positions are most often evaluated with quite secular rather than spiritual standards.

One who is suitable for membership on the staff team often lacks the "flavor" and the "heat" of genuine discipleship. What is worse, denominational staff people are often suspicious of those who exhibit the marks of a profound spiritual orientation. Therefore, we have largely excluded the most effective clergy and lay people from consideration for staff positions, and this has given us a kind of wholesale spiritual mediocrity in many of our denominational staffs.

From my experience those who appoint staff members often

reject applicants with exemplary abilities and gifts because "they simply would not fit in." A "salt and fire" staff person would have a hard time coöperating with the shallow and cowardly approaches to church problems so often used by denominational officials and staff members. Several denominational staff people I have known who possessed profound spiritual depth and outstanding abilities were fired with the explanation, "They were very competent but they just were not team members."

In some instances that might be a valid complaint, but all too often the gifted and dedicated people dropped from denominational staffs were *too* strongly endowed with spiritual qualities. Not only do these Christians not fit in, they are often seen as threats. The contrast with existing staff members is too obvious. They are not good for "staff morale" because one of the typical traits of "little foxes" is jealousy.

Sadly, there is as much professional jealousy among clergy as there is among other professionals. Jesus promised his followers that if they were true to his message they would inevitably meet with severe opposition and persecution. "Remember the word that I said to you, 'Servants are not greater than their master.' If they persecuted me, they will persecute you" *(Jn 15:20)*.

Denominational representatives characteristically forget Jesus' mandate when they deal with pastors who encounter opposition from their members. They do not entertain the assumption that pastors who are true to their calling will receive severe opposition and persecution, but most often assume that good "professionalism" avoids such difficulties.

Sometimes there are situations of conflict between congregations and their pastors in which the pastors are at fault, so very honest and careful assessments need to be made to determine where the blame is. But my experience is that this happens infrequently. The local church leaders and the designated denominational staff person usually meet and hear both sides of the conflict in a "going through the motions" fashion, and the result is most often that the pastor is terminated or assigned to another pastorate to avoid personality conflicts.

I once heard David Buttrick, professor of homiletics at Vanderbilt Divinity School, point out an interesting contradiction in the reactions of many clergy to denominational leaders and staffs. He said a widespread opinion among many pastors and prominent Christian scholars is that denominational staffs too often operate with the wrong priorities. We also often bemoan the fact that our denominations are dying. "Leave them alone and let them die," Buttrick said, "and everyone will be better off!"

The remark is pretty harsh, but I have to admit I find a degree of merit in it. The death of denominations, or the death of their adverse, bureaucratic methods, would mean we would have a much better chance of unity among Christian communions, and the pooling of our financial, material, and human resources would mean more for evangelism including mission work.

The death of denominations or their radical reform would also mean the death of the authority façade. Denominational staffs function under a bureaucratic façade. Obviously this is not as much the case with churches with an episcopal polity, but even bishops have only as much authority as their constituents are willing to give them.

The authority façade is responsible for the problem that exists when denominational staff people try to deal with conflicts between pastors and members of their congregations. If pastors are guilty of serious, unethical or immoral behavior, they are usually disciplined by the appropriate body of the denomination. However when a faithful pastor is harassed by a congregation, the complaining members are not rebuked. It would seem that the only reason for this lack of authority and courage in support of pastors who have been mistreated is because it protects the churches' financial contributions to the denomination.

Immediately following my meeting with the local church and ministry committee in Connecticut that heard from me and from my representatives about my imminent departure and the reasons for it, the regional conference minister turned to the officers of the church to help with the process of calling a new pastor. Our family had not even started packing yet! The characteristic denominational approach to local congregation problems that are spiritual in nature is to gloss over them with statements like "just a bad match" or "a difference in style." They seemingly do not realize that the real problems remain, inevitably to rise to the surface again.

Leaders may whitewash over the problems, but Scriptures warn us, "There will be a deluge of rain, great hailstones will fall, and a stormy wind will break out. When the wall falls, will it not be said to you, 'Where is the whitewash you smeared on it?'" *(Ez 13:11b-12)*. We are seeing in our times the death of denominationalism for the same reasons that most "isms" are not lasting: they are not healthy and productive enough to attract enthusiastic support. A large "apostate" kingdom has been formed. One insightful preacher has said: "The kingdom of Saul is falling and the kingdom of David is being built."

This idea should not surprise Christians, because Christian faith was born from the death of a unique but limited human being in the interest of an unlimited and universal presence of the Holy Spirit *(Jn. 16:14ff)*. The death of the mainline denominations in their present form is that kind of sacrifice, not in the sense of sinless atonement as Christ's was, but in the sense of sacrificing church organizations that have grown dear to many of us.

But denominations do not necessarily have to cease existing. They could reform their errors and weaknesses. The "apostasy," the impersonal relationship with God, the absence of the Holy Spirit's profound residence in people, the wrong priorities, and the other liabilities we have talked about have the marks of a strategic, intelligent design. They are the experiences and methods that have been proven to be so destructive for the evangelism and church growth in our congregations.

The demise of our denominations could be avoided by their turning around and correcting the adverse conditions they have fallen into. At some point denominational officers and representatives of local congregations could grow so concerned about the persistent downsizing of their congregations and denominations that renewal would be seen as their only hope. Frankly, however, given their past experience, I do not hold out much hope for this eventuality.

Whatever course this fatal trend takes, it is imperative that we include the renewal of denominations in any effort to renew the church. Currently they are the largest bastions *against* the church's renewal in our time.

"Lord, These denominational organizations appear as "giants in the land" to us. We are no match for them, but we know they are not giants to you. Lord, please lead us in the way of renewal for them. Amen."

16

Let's Go!

Go therefore and make disciples of all nations, baptizing them in the name of the Father and of the Son and of the Holy Spirit (Mt 28:19).

The operative word in the Great Commission is *go*. For at least 18 centuries the Christian church has sent its representatives everywhere in the world. For most of those years there was a continual stream of new Christians forged into many local congregations. In countless places throughout the world, the quality of human life has been radically enriched by the church to a degree unequaled by any other organization, institution, or agency because Christians heard the command to go and they went.

Attendance at worship and membership in our churches has been steadily declining since the early 1950s. As the church was nearing the end of the 20th Century, the United Church of Christ, for one, was losing 50 metropolitan churches each year and it is by no means the only denomination experiencing major decline. Mission work in every mainline Protestant denomination has also been severely reduced as a result of declining income and changes in vision.

This decline is not due altogether to the church's spiritual condition or lack of commitment, but in large measure it is a re-

What's the Matter with the Church?

sult of the cultural changes that have led to fewer people interested in church life. One of the major influences has been the demographics that seem to have had a tremendous impact on church involvement, not only in America but also in the other industrial nations of the world though most of my observations relate to what has been happening to the church in America.

As the automobile came into its own in the 1920s and 30s, so increasingly, working-class people were able to buy cars and gain a new mobility. World War II caused a cessation of automobile manufacturing, but soon after the war it resumed with a much larger market than ever before. A family that owned a car could now move much further away from their work place and from public transportation lines to newer and more spacious communities. Those without cars were left in the central cities where many of the jobs were low income.

Mainline denominational churches had never been populated with a host of poor people, so most of the residents who were left in the central cities found it even more difficult to find church homes in these congregations, but this migration caused many of the churches in the central cities to begin a severe decline. While America's transportation revolution was still cresting, the church took another serious hit—television. With such absorbing entertainment right in their own living rooms, people became far less inclined to attend worship services and Sunday school. Added to these developments was a population growth rate unmatched in previous years, so even if church participation had remained a constant, our evangelism outreach would be inadequate.

But while social changes can account for fewer members in city congregations, they do not explain the complete reversal from a condition of gaining members to one of losing them. Over the years I have become convinced these sociological developments were not the root cause of the decline. Rather it appears to me that serious Christian discipleship became less popular in most churches long ago. How far back it is difficult to tell. My personal experience with the church in the 1950s left me with the memory that by then did not have any significant number of genuine evangelical witnesses who went out to find unchurched people to share the gospel with nor to invite to their churches. Church membership and participation in those years was due mostly to the religious inclinations of that time, which are quite different from those in our time.

So if the church had been populated with disciples who were intentional about sharing the gospel with people, and had it been organizing evangelism programs during the years when the church was growing, it would obviously have grown more than it did. More of the new Christians would have been genuine disciples, because they would not have been involved in church life mainly as a result of social interest or family tradition. Had authentic Christian discipleship been the dominant commitment in those years our churches in our time, numerical growth would still be happening.

Rarely today do we find that any of the new members in churches are joining because they have had a profound experience with Jesus Christ that brings them into a personal relationship with him. It is apparent that for the most part the churches that are adding members are not doing much evangelism either. Most additions to our church families come by transfer of their membership from other churches, and most of the ones who come by profession of faith have actually just decided at some point that church membership would be a good thing for them; another reason that very little "salt" and "fire" permeates our congregations.

We have long since settled down. We have not been reaching out for a long time. Nothing could be clearer than the fact that Jesus invited his followers to join a movement, not just an institution, but early in its history this movement became an institution. Admittedly, this institution has done and continues to do much good in the world, but most of the great works of the church were done by those who had a movement mentality. There is nothing wrong with the movement being organized and building buildings for its meetings and other functions, but when this happens to a movement, it becomes institutionalized. It is worth noting that the Christian movement, historically, did not build any buildings for the first 170 years, during which period it accomplished getting the Gospel preached on all the continents and in most of the cultures of the world.

Such a "movement" doesn't have to get lost in an institution if its members are careful to prevent it. Early in its history members of the movement most likely did not see the importance of vigorously opposing the institutional mentality. Down through the years I have met people in almost every church I have attended or served who have a movement mentality, but sadly enough they are in the very small minority.

The analogy of theater seating to the church has been often employed because it is such an apt statement. Most members of our churches are not actors on the stage as they should be but are members of the audience, observers of the action. Beyond these are those who remain in the balcony even farther from the show.

Most church members are interested bystanders, not involved in the ministry and mission of the church beyond its worship services. Few demonstrate they have the "salt" or the "fire" nor give any indication they have that hunger for scriptures in which its words become the Word, words through which the Holy Spirit gives authentic life as Paul tells us: "The letter kills but the Spirit gives life" *(2 Co 3:6)*. No wonder they lack a rich commitment to personal witnessing. Since they are not motivated to forgo much personal convenience, they are unwilling to part with much of their resources to finance the ministries of the church.

There is no evidence that Jesus had an audience, much less a balcony, in his mind when he called people to follow him, and he invited and challenged his listeners to become disciples, not members of an institution. In many churches, we have all but abandoned its missional character. The task of renewal would necessarily and basically involve getting mission churches going again.

Also important for our task of evangelism and missions is that we see clearly the relationship between suffering and "salvation." People who are suffering are far more eager to receive the Gospel than those who are more or less comfortable.

For many years I did not understand why so many of the Gospel accounts deal with the healing ministry of Jesus. Finally, through my experiences in counseling I figured it out. I have had the opportunity of helping a number of people come into a personal relationship with Christ, or to come into a closer one with him, because they were suffering so much they were willing to accept that kind of counsel and take it seriously.

I have learned much from the fields of psychiatry and psychology, especially the immeasurable value of "creative listening" rather than the giving of advice. But proposing ways counselees can come to know Jesus Christ or strengthen their relationship with him is definitely counseling of the finest sort.

Pain and suffering are such strong motivators that they move us when nothing else will to accept suggested relief. We should seek to minister to people who are suffering severe difficulties and share with them our experience with Christ, suggesting that in the fellowship of Christ's church they can find answers to their most basic problems. This is also why two of the church's primary ministries comprise the greater part of its main calling – sharing the gospel especially with the poor and assisting suffering people, which we should do anyway out of Christian love. The church's evangelism to suffering people is based on both of the two main marching orders of the church. Jesus was very clear it was a waste of time to try to share the Word of God's grace with people who think they are "healthy." It is not they, he said, who need a doctor, but the sick *(Mk 2:17)*.

If we are to be true to our calling, we will find who and where suffering people are in our community and go to them, assisting them where we can and making sure we share the gospel with them in a very self-conscious way if they have not accepted God's saving grace in Jesus Christ. Again the operative word is *go*.

We can invite these people to come visit our church, we can

spend great sums of money on putting invitational advertisements in newspapers and in other media, but in the final analysis this kind of "marketing" does not motivate many of the suffering and poor to come to our churches. I have rarely found that people respond to advertisements by visiting our worship services. The poor, for the most part, feel out of place and are uncomfortable in our denominational churches, so their embarrassment tends to prevent them from visiting our services. It is the saddest of commentaries that millions of poor people attend worship every Sunday and many other ministries during the week, but comparatively few of these choose to join denominational churches.

Going to the poor just to "deliver" the Christian message to them has never been very effective. Instead of saying, "We have the bread you need," we should rather think of ourselves as one poor beggar telling another beggar where to find bread.

The sharing of a personal relationship with God in Jesus Christ cannot be done with much depth and richness in an impersonal relationship. Salespeople have been on to this principle for ages. "You have to sell yourself first" is their commonplace dictum. So, too, a personal relationship needs to be developed to some degree between the person who is sharing the Good News and the person with whom they are sharing it.

A personal relationship does not necessarily require a lot of time to develop. It is a *matter* of the person who is the object of our testimony perceiving a personal quality in the attitude of the witness. Some people come off to others with a personal quality immediately; for some it takes time, but for others it never happens. "Witnessing" is not a persuasive argument; it is a sharing of one's experience, which cannot be done in the abstract. It is like sharing a piece of music on paper with someone. They can see the notes, but as important as that is at times, it is no substitute for hearing the music.

This was always a special problem for Judaism. It is very difficult to make sharing God's Law personal. It is a strong witness to the uniqueness of Christian faith that it has been difficult if not impossible for all other religious traditions. But God became a person in Jesus Christ, who himself possessed to a phenomenal degree a quality that was instantly intuited by people who met him.

The saving grace of God in Jesus Christ is a free, unmerited gift. Our witnessing, therefore, is the sharing of a gift, and a genuine gift cannot be sincerely shared with anyone by someone who acts in any way "superior". Regardless of one's station in society, a genuine gift can only be given by one who has a peer attitude toward the person to whom the gift is offered. Social and financial standing, although strong influences in human relationships, are not the determinants of one's peer attitude toward others. Wealthy people sometimes have a personal attitude toward poor people and then the latter are treated as equals, while on the other hand the communications of poor people to others who are poor sometimes come across as abstract and impersonal. It is the attitude that *matters*, and it is obvious that we cannot have a personal relationship with people if we insist they come to us. We must go to them.

The primary mission of the church is evangelism, and that term refers to people accepting God's forgiveness and Jesus Christ as their savior and Lord. It does not refer to those who just join a church or transfer their membership. Real evangelism has been all but eliminated in the ministries of many churches and in most denominational churches. An effort to renew evangelism requires radical attitudinal change on the part of both laity and clergy. This cannot be accomplished by a program that does not change our members' attitudes.

"Lord, Please save us from brushing aside the needed changes in your church as though they do not exist. Help us to face them honestly and thereby realize how immense the difficulty involved is in changing them, and how utterly we are dependent upon you for accomplishing any measure of the task. Amen."

17

More than a Feeling

Little children, let us love, not in word or speech, but in truth and action (1 Jn 3:18).

Unconditional love has become a very popular concept. We encounter it in secular contexts as well as in church circles, but what is not widely known is that Jesus introduced this concept of love into human history. There is no trace of it before he spoke of it in reference to the love God has for us. Only God is capable of love that is completely unconditional, love that does not depend upon the behavior of its object, that has no element of deserving, that is given to people in spite of what they are or do. Jesus' practice was to exhort people with perfectionistic standards, so he held up unconditional love, *agape*, as the standard for caring about others.

The highest form of love to which people have ever been challenged was given to the world by the church's New Testament. (It is important to remember that the New Testament did not produce the church, as it is commonly thought; the church produced The New Testament.)

Love is somehow referred to in nearly all sermons preached in Christian churches, and the impact on the world with the idea that love should be the fundamental ethic in human relations has come more from the church than from any other source. It stands to reason then that much of the love in the world, if not most, has been generated by the church. Also, the church has spread hosts of loving acts toward people throughout the world. Representatives of the church have acted in countless instances on behalf of people who had no other advocates.

One of the main reasons, however, for the church's "apostasy" is a widespread misunderstanding of what love is. The love Jesus spoke about was far different from the ways the word is used in secular society. Genuine caring seems to be at the heart of what Jesus meant by the term he used. What constitutes genuine love even at the levels of which humans are capable, is seen primarily as an emotion, but authentic love is far more than a feeling.

In the summary of my systematic theology, *Caring Is God*, my argument for the ultimacy of caring is based on its existence on all three levels of human experience, body, mind, and emotions as seen in the facility of the term's common usage on all three levels. We speak of caring about someone as a feeling, "He cares for his girlfriend." We refer to the level of the body when we say things like "Nurses care for their patients." We use the word on the level of the mind when we speak of doing something "carefully."

This provides us with a way of seeing the comprehensive nature of caring as it relates to our relationships with others. Love is not just a feeling. That is just one-third of what love is, and the lesser important one at that. Genuine love also means being willing to care for the physical needs of others when we are given the opportunity to care for them in appropriate ways (food, clothing, housing, health and sex). The third dimension of love means doing whatever we do for them carefully. We can hurt people when we think we are loving them if we are not careful.

This explains Jesus' commandment to love. The feeling of love cannot be commanded. You cannot get people to feel love for others by commanding them to do it. To the degree that love is an action, and two out of the three dimensions of personhood have to do with action, it can be commanded.

Just because we sat in worship services or attend other inspirational experiences and feel love for the poor, distressed or sick in our midst, that is not enough to be called Christian love. For it to be Christian caring we must add the careful planning of the right way to help them and actually do something for them.

Do people like the poor, the minorities or gay people get the idea that we love them if we send them goods and services and yet make it unmistakable in other ways they are not really welcome at our church services and other activities? Do we really think we love them when we assault their feelings in this way? Much of our church talk about loving people is ludicrous. We too often talk about something that makes us feel good, but does nothing for the people we say we love. So much of the "love" we see among church people does not even approach unconditional, nor is it even genuine, even in the traditional sense of the word.

The charge we hear most against the church by people outside its fellowships is that its members are hypocrites. I believe the reason this accusation is made so often is because people outside the church know we talk about love a great deal, but they do not see us doing much about it. Those who have critical needs and are in severe crises have no need for our feelings of love. We can only help meet their needs if we do something for them boldly and carefully. I have long been struck with the titles of John Bisagno's book, *Love Is Something We Do*. This is the deciding issue for love. The renewal of the church means its members begin to love much more in "deed and in truth." Nothing *matters* more in the life and ministry of the church.

Where it exists, this failing of the church is a serious failing indeed. Our Lord told us he would consider our behavior toward other people as if it were done to him.

> All the nations will be gathered before him, and he will separate people one from another as a shepherd separates the sheep from the goats, and he will put the sheep at his right hand and the goats at the left. Then the king will say to those at his right

hand, "Come, you that are blessed by my Father, inherit the kingdom prepared for you from the foundation of the world; for I was hungry and you gave me food, I was thirsty and you gave me something to drink, I was a stranger and you welcomed me, I was naked and you gave me clothing, I was sick and you took care of me, I was in prison and you visited me." Then the righteous will answer him, 'Lord, when was it that we saw you hungry and gave you food, or thirsty and gave you something to drink? And when was it that we saw you a stranger and welcomed you, or naked and gave you clothing? And when was it that we saw you sick or in prison and visited you?" And the king will answer them, "Truly I tell you, just as you did it to one of the least of these who are members of my family, you did it to me." Then he will say to those at his left hand, "You that are accursed, depart from me into the eternal fire prepared for the devil and his angels; for I was hungry and you gave me no food, I was thirsty and you gave me nothing to drink, I was a stranger and you did not welcome me, naked and you did not give me clothing, sick and in prison and you did not visit me." Then they also will answer, "Lord, when was it that we saw you hungry or thirsty or a stranger or naked or sick or in prison, and did not take care of you?" Then he will answer them, "Truly I tell you, just as you did not do it to one of the least of these, you did not do it to me." And these will go away into eternal punishment, but the righteous into eternal life *(Mt 25:32-46)*.

Now that's very serious talk! Just imagine all the people in our churches who get no further with love than the sentimental feeling. We have to assume they are not aware of the seriousness of their sin. What is worse, how often have you heard this failing confronted honestly enough to convict people about it?

Regardless of what we say about loving Jesus, the way we show our love for him is by keeping his commandments. "If you love me, you will keep my commandments" *(Jn 14:15)*. There is no question about Jesus commanding us to love. He understood the whole Hebrew law in terms of loving God and loving our neighbor as we love ourselves, and he was surely not talking about our feelings. How many in our congregations, therefore, would have to say their actions do not show much love for him?

Given this widespread shortcoming of the church, it is no wonder the church has fallen into decline in numbers, in influence, and in spiritual power. Nothing is more basic to the church's mission than this. Nothing *matters* more. And nothing is more the *matter* with the church than this. For the renewal of the church love in action is a must. We can safely say that to the degree that this condition is not shown, other areas cannot be renewed.

18

Killing the Bear

"If we do not go outside and kill the bear, the bear will come into the house and kill us" (Old Russian proverb).

The Church once held such authority for social issues, and almost everything else as well, that people, including monarchs and rulers of nations, were hard-pressed to disobey its pronouncements. Autocratic authority was not the kind of power it should have had, but we have come all the way from this role of total authority to one of virtually none at all. Whatever authority any church still appears to have does nor include the power to demand compliance with doctrine. As soon as members disagree with a position or a teaching of the church, the façade of authority disappears. Pastors and church leaders rarely make any effort to enforce conformity to its standards.

In the 1950s and '60s major denominations and their pastors took many supportive stands on critical social issues, but as the opposition of its members to these positions mounted, shown by withholding funds and withdrawing membership by individuals, or in some cases by whole congregations, pastors all began to backtrack on social issues. Soon the usual position was standing up for Christian convictions on social issues as long as there wasn't too much opposition. Seldom do we hear pastors and denominational leaders speak out today on controversial social issues, and when we do, it is done with so much "tact" it makes no one uncomfortable.

We have gone from preaching the radical Gospel of Jesus Christ, to preaching a "tactful" gospel. This is to me the clearest expression of the prevailing cowardice of the contemporary church. In our time, we have to admit, the church often had a decisive influence on many local and national questions, but now it tends to avoid the kind of controversial stands the Hebrew prophets and our Lord took about society and it's ecclesiastical and political leaders.

> Thus says the Lord: For three transgressions of Judah, and for four, I will not revoke the punishment; because they sell the righteous for silver, and the needy for a pair of sandals – they who trample the head of the poor into the dust of the earth, and push the afflicted out of the way; father and son go into the same girl, so that my holy name is profaned; they lay themselves down beside every altar on garments taken in pledge; and in the house of their God they drink wine bought with fines they imposed *(Am 2:6-8).*
>
> At that very hour some Pharisees came and said to him, "Get away from here, for Herod wants to kill you." He said to them, "Go and tell that fox for me, "Listen, I am casting out demons and performing cures today and tomorrow, and on the third day I finish my work *(Lk 13:31-32).*

The civil-rights movement of the 1960s stands as the last great social witness of the church, dramatically demonstrating what social power the church has when it is released. Many feel the civil-rights movement was the most important social change in 20th Century America, and it inspired progress in social justice in almost every country in the world. It would never have come about had it not been for the Christian church for it was begun by Black Christians, mainly promoted by Black church members, and supported by white and minority members of mainline denominational churches. Its leader, Dr. Martin Luther King, Jr., was a young Black pastor from Atlanta serving a church in Birmingham,

Alabama, when the movement exploded onto the main stage of human events. It was, therefore, essentially a church movement.

Like thousands of others, I joined the civil-rights campaigns in Alabama and Mississippi. One of my lasting memories from those days is of meeting elderly white people and others on the marches who were not typical members or supporters of social movements. Invariably they would tell me they were from such-and-such a city or town and such-and-such a church. I was constantly amazed at this and I have never been prouder of being part of the Christian church. I had never realized the church was capable of such historic social greatness. It would be a tragic loss if this greatness was never to be seen again in the church's life.

There was, however, a great deal of controversy throughout the church over the civil-rights movement. Social issues often cause heated differences of opinions when they are raised in the church. This has been a difficult arena for the church's ministry around our country. It is hard to know how the church needs to address controversial issues since actions and positions people take on them can become so divisive in congregations and denominations.

Escapism from the world has always had a strong presence in the church, but fortunately, the church's social witness and ministry, if significantly diminished, has tenaciously persisted. Many of our churches and all of the major denominations have departments and committees charged with focusing the attention of their communions on these issues and providing leadership in addressing them. We do not have to create these structures; they just need to be renewed.

But as troubled a road as addressing social concerns has been for the church, we cannot in good conscience avoid ignoring important social concerns, as many pastors and churches have chosen to do. It is a road of Christian conscience we must go down, and one we have not traveled nearly far enough.

The church's need to address some social questions is a must, if for no other reason than because it is crucial for the health of the church that we do it. We should keep in mind that going into the world to work for or against certain social conditions often involves issues that play important roles in making our society more or less favorable to the church's message and ministries.

There is another important reason the church should stand against injustice and immorality. We have an obligation to encourage our members in Christian social attitudes, positions and actions because if we don't go into the world and oppose these evils, as the old Russian proverb has it, "The bear will come into the house and kill us." Social values, priorities and practices have a way of influencing our members. At a time when evangelism is reaping such poor results, it seems to me "the world has come into the church far more than the church has gone into the world."

Trying to insulate the church from the world is not an effective way to prevent negative attitudes and values from infecting our members. In the first place, it is impossible to do. Our members participate in countless ways in wider society. There is no effective way to insulate them from it. What is needed is an aggressive ministry against those elements before they take up residence in the minds of the members of our churches.

There are no better examples of the "killing the bear" phenomena than two conditions that scandalized the church during the time I was working on these essays: President Bill Clinton had a sexual affair with a young intern in the White House and Republican party leaders began a frantic and unrelenting campaign to impeach him. The fanatical special prosecutor (maybe "persecutor" would be a more fitting title), Ken Starr, had his so called "case" on television every day and had truckloads of documents delivered to the Congress detailing the affair in the most graphic, salacious details of.

Never has there been a more outrageous legal maneuver than when he put all these details on the internet and in the newspapers for the public to read, including children! Republican spokespersons took whatever opportunity they could to get their angry charges against Clinton on the news channels. It was nauseating to watch Starr give his accounts of the legal process with his phony expressions of objectivity and deadpan insistence that this was not "personal" or "political" with him.

But my point is that the biggest scandal was not Clinton's dalliance. It was the church's silence in the *matter*. I did not hear a whisper from any mainline church representatives. There were many angry denunciations and moral and religious condemnations from fundamentalist preachers and television evangelists. Do you suppose none of these preachers were familiar enough with the New Testament to have read Jesus' story about the adulteress and the rock throwers? Were they unaware that Jesus condemned the rock throwers, not the adulteress? What Bible have they been reading lately? Obviously, their political prejudice was what blinded them.

But mainline preachers and denominational spokespersons are intelligent enough to have known about Jesus' memorable parable. Surely at least some of them made the connection, but we heard not a word. I wish I could think of a less serious failure of our mission to society, but only cowardice on a huge scale can account for it.

The second large scandal involves an ultraconservative president who was not elected by a popular vote and maybe not even by an electoral college vote, since he used the courts to keep all the votes from being counted. Of course he claimed there was no need to count the same votes over and over again, but that was obviously to distract from the fact that thousands of votes were not counted at all. Rather than being elected, he was "selected" by one Republican supreme court justice, and he assumed office with no measure of humility for not having been chosen by the people, but with an arrogance that belies the attitude that he has a mandate. So far not a word from the church.

That president, while ignoring the lack of support from the U.N., the organization that was created largely due to the United States' leadership, has impetuously taken the country into a war of invasion and occupation which at the time of this writing, has cost almost two thousand American lives and continues to add great numbers to the ranks of the terrorists and of our enemies in the world. Even though he admits he used fallacious documents to stir up fear in the country so that many would follow him to war, still no word has come from the church.

Whatever happened to that church I came to respect so much for its loud voice of social witness and its sending thousands of its members into the streets demanding justice and civil rights for minorities and the end of a horribly wrong war? "Where have all the flowers gone?" Where is its witness now? We may find it painful to admit it, but it simply does not exist.

The most disturbing situation in the current state of affairs is that pollsters have discovered that most Americans who attend church support the political conservatives, this shameful president, his war and his reëlection, and that most Americans who support liberal politicians and ideas do not attend church. Zogby, a Muslim, and one of the four or five leading pollsters in the country said he was baffled by this because it was evident to him that liberal views are far more consistent with the teachings of Jesus than are conservative views.

Could it be? O, Lord, could it be? Please let me suggest to you the horrible possibility that the "bear" has invaded the church to the extent that it has totally converted it and that enemies of the Truth now populate the pews so that the followers of Jesus Christ's ideals are more likely to be found outside the walls of our churches. How else can this situation be explained? What worse predicament can be imagined than this?

We cannot let the church off the hook with the excuse that strong ministry is a divisive force in our congregations and denominations. There are many social issues in our country and our communities that are not controversial at all among our members: hunger, education, crime, healthcare, elderly and children's services, and many more. Yet even on these safe issues the church does not have a very aggressive ministry.

But there is a ministry that needs to be addressed prior to getting the church to play a more active role in social questions.

A much more serious problem underlying how we deal with social issues is that we have never spent much time teaching the members of our congregations to respond to differences of opinion among them in loving tolerance. The main emphasis for renewal of the church's social concerns ministry should be placed on getting our members to realize and demonstrate that a spirit of love and freedom prevails in the church as a chosen lifestyle. A congregation in which people treat others with whom they disagree with cheerful affection and cordial respect has a much stronger witness to Christian faith in its community than does a congregation where expressed disagreements are not tolerated.

Jesus pointed out that we don't have to have the love of God to be kind and caring to people with whom we agree. "Even the gentiles" do that, he said *(Mt 5:47)*. People with no spiritual commitment at all are perfectly capable of tolerance. Christian love comes into play when we relate to people who hold strongly opposite views to ours. For the church to bear witness effectively as a community of faith where love overlays all our differences of opinion would be as great a gift to our society as anything imaginable. Our society needs this example desperately.

Since the Vietnam war, our country has been riddled with continual controversies in which people on one side of an issue have been hostile to those on the other. Our world could benefit immensely from the example of people who hold conflicting opinions but who share a community of faith and love, and who forge ministries of reconciliation to those involved in controversies. This is a far greater need than is the need for the church as a body to take sides in the public arguments.

A pastor's attempt to deal with these issues needs to be strongly flavored with love. One of my frequent failings in dealing with these *matters* is that too often I have not communicated my convictions with a loving spirit. St. Paul's admonishment to make sure we are "speaking the truth in love" *(Ep 4:15)* is of primary importance when we are dealing with people who disagree with us. The apostle promises us a reward of great consequence for practicing this principle:

> "We must no longer be children, tossed to and fro and blown about by every wind of doctrine, by people's trickery, by their craftiness in deceitful scheming. But speaking the truth in love, we must grow up in every way into him who is the head, into Christ, from whom the whole body, joined and knit together by every ligament with which it is equipped, as each part is working properly, promotes the body's growth in building itself up in love *(Ep 4:14-16)*.

I can think of no greater reward than to be matured in Christ, to be built up in love, to have the whole congregation strengthened and fortified in love with each part of its mission and ministry increased. Just our speaking the truth in love (and both parts—the truth and love—are indispensable) will bring about more renewal, perhaps, than anything else.

We hope this will be so often done that we have renewal going on almost everywhere, and it is happening in some congregations. It is, however, not happening nearly as much as it should, because while we are big on speaking in love we are woefully short on "speaking the truth." Because we are afraid of controversial reactions, it is not often we see pastors and people lovingly, but boldly, holding up the church's social witness.

Pastors should be very careful when they deal with these issues. If they avoid controversial issues in their sermons for lack of courage, it is not a good thing; but if they deal with them tactfully, or even at times avoid them out of practical and caring wisdom, it is a good thing. There are times when pastors should have the courage to confront their congregations with truths that may make some members angry. Here the principle of practical wisdom should not be used in those instances to let pastors "get off the hook," but every attempt should be made to make their statements as palatable as possible.

It is a distinguishing mark of pastors with genuine "heart" that they are able to broach potentially divisive subjects in ways that promote the least anger. An artful pastor does not shy away from stands that may be controversial, and neither does one shove them in the faces of his listeners with inflammatory statements. The decision to deal with a question of this kind should be guided by the "salt and fire," the prayerful and earnest seeking for the leadership of the Spirit.

There are keen subtleties here. How can pastors know if what they want to say on an issue that might be factious is motivated by courage and spiritual wisdom or by arrogance, willfulness, or anger? Human wisdom alone is woefully subjective and untrustworthy for these situations. We can be wrong about them even when we seek the guidance of the Spirit, because even this effort is also fraught with our finiteness and subjectivity. The problem's of what stands we should take on these issues are much too subtle and complex for human understanding.

In the recent years of my pastoral experience I have come to conclude, rather surprisingly for me, that for the most part I have no right to preach my social concerns if my stands brings division within the congregation. My opinions, even my convictions, about social issues should not be important enough to me to unduly "push" them from the pulpit. If I try to persuade some members of the congregation, or argue with them about these *matters*, I am simply taking one side of an argument among my members against the other, and that is a far cry from preaching the Gospel.

We would do well to remember often how Paul begged the Ephesians to keep unity foremost among them "making every effort to maintain the unity of the Spirit in the bond of peace" *(Ep 4:3)*. This is not a unity of sacrificed or compromised convictions; it is not a unity in which members refuse to express their opinions, nor, in fact, a unity that is maintained by human effort at all. It is a unity of the Spirit held by all the members under the guidance and direction of God's Spirit that requires their relating to one another and their mission in humility and love. They are to be held together not by protection of their opposing opinions but by the "bond of peace."

> I therefore, the prisoner in the Lord, beg you to lead a life wor-
> thy of the calling to which you have been called, with all humil-
> ity and gentleness, with patience, bearing with one another in
> love, making every effort to maintain the unity of the Spirit in
> the bond of peace *(Ep 4:3)*.

This is a beautiful vision of Christian fellowship, but in practical terms how do we attain it? To begin with, in most cases, only
those issues that find unity among the members of the church
should be advocated from the pulpit. Those that are disputable
should be the private domain of individuals who seek to see them
in the light of the Gospel, or that of special ministry groups in the
church. The attitude that should prevail is one that sees the opposing opinions of other church members as views that can be de-
bated with "smiles on our faces," in positive, good-natured, kind,
and even humorous terms. There is no good reason why Christians who share the same local, denominational, or interdenomina-
tional fellowship cannot conduct themselves according to these
standards. What is required is that they subordinate their individual views to the leadership of the Spirit.

This is easier said than done because we are dealing in these
matters with the heart of human sinfulness, selfishness, which
above all else needs transformation by Christ. There should always
be evidence of our strenuous efforts and practice at doing this. It
is a *matter* of trying to put the "kingdom of God first." It is not
something we can accomplish in this life, and we are not required
to accomplish it, but we are exhorted by Christ to seek it. And for
seeking it we will reap an incomparable reward. "But strive first
for the kingdom of God and his righteousness, and all these things
will be given to you as well" *(Mt 6:33)*. While this is a challenging
discipline, there is a compelling motivation to maintain it.

Humility on the part of pastors is of utmost importance. It is
helpful when pastors, trying to address one of these social questions, actually apologizes for their own errors on the subject. This
usually minimizes the defensiveness on the part of the listeners and
mitigates their tendency to become angry or to feel like the pastor

is using the pulpit to "beat them over the head."

And in dealing with these kinds of issues, pastors always need to flavor their humility with love. That is why Paul insists on our not living "in the futility" of our own thinking. "Now this I affirm and insist on in the Lord: you must no longer live as the Gentiles live, in the futility of their minds" *(Ep 4:17)*. Nothing is as futile as relying on the triumph of our opinions. We obviously come closer to God's wisdom and truth when we express our convictions in love and humility.

Jesus' instruction to his followers to be "separate from the world" has been used frequently to avoid the church's social responsibilities, but his exhortation to be in the world but not of the world informs this issue. We must be in the world because we have been sent into the world, as Jesus' prayer for his followers in the Gospel of John makes clear: "As you have sent me into the world, so I have sent them into the world" *(Jn 17:18)*. So we are to be in the world out of obedience, but not to be of this world. We are not to be guided by the values, priorities, interests or styles of the world.

In order to speak to people outside the church, we should on occasion adopt some styles and modes of the world, as long as these do not conflict with Christian values. But the quality and direction of our lives are to be determined by the values that are advocated and shown by our Lord. This means our fellowship is to be very different from the world, and this is to be clearly evident to people who observe it from the outside.

We have some serious problems on this score. Most of the members of our congregations, both the poor and the wealthy, have been infected by the world's obsession with materialism and social status. Anyone who has experience with most any Christian church can hardly miss the deference with which wealthy people are favored by pastors and members. People outside the church see this and conclude that we are not different from any other group of people.

We cannot be effective Christian witnesses to our neighbors

What's the Matter with the Church?

if we have no personal involvement with them. When the prophet Ezekiel sought a ministry among his people in captivity, he wisely chose to "sit where they sat." "Then I came to the captives at Tel Abib, who dwelt by the River Chebar; and I sat where they sat, and remained there astonished among them seven days" (Ez 3:15).

We frequently miss evangelistic opportunities of great promise because we do not–personally–get involved enough with the people to whom we seek to minister. When we really have a ministry of social concerns, we often have it in partnership with people outside the church. We get to know them and they develop favorable impressions of us because we agree on the issue involved. This is a fertile field for our witness. Just think, if all our churches were involved in the lively issues of the nation and their communities, we would discover a field so "plentiful" we would need to recruit far more people to work in it. "Then he said to his disciples, 'The harvest is plentiful, but the laborers are few; therefore ask the Lord of the harvest to send out laborers into his harvest'" (Mt 9:37-38).

Even though the harvest is plentiful, we don't see the world that way because we keep going over the fields that have been harvested decades ago. The field of social concerns is one of those yet unharvested "plentiful" fields. To bring renewal to the church's social concerns ministry is a big order. It needs to begin with intentional, educational and consciousness-raising efforts at the local church level, effects that include an emphasis on encouraging members with different opinions to keep their relationships positive and their expressions kind.

We have been "sent" into the world, but we are not really in the world unless we have a difference-making presence in the discussions of its most highly charged issues. We cannot conduct our ministry in the social concerns and action arenas unless we are bound by the unity of the Spirit, which is the unity of love and humility.

19

Born for Trouble

And what more should I say? For time would fail me to tell of Gideon, Barak, Samson, Jephthah, of David and Samuel and the prophets—who through faith conquered kingdoms, administered justice, obtained promises, shut the mouths of lions, quenched raging fire, escaped the edge of the sword, won strength out of weakness, became mighty in war, put foreign armies to flight (Heb 11:32-34).

The Detroit riots erupted in the summer of 1967 when I was serving as pastor of the First Congregational church of Dearborn, Michigan, a Detroit suburb. An ad hoc group called the Interfaith Action Council was called into being by church leaders of several denominations. It was made up of pastors, denominational executives, representatives from city and county governments, police officials and the business and labor communities. A crisis center was established at the Episcopal diocesan headquarters and seminary near the city's central area because the occupants had vacated the facility when disturbances erupted a few blocks away and the diocese had offered their building to the council for emergency operations.

When I called the United Church of Christ conference office in Detroit to ask how I could help, they told me about the council, so I drove downtown to the center and volunteered to help in any way I could. I was invited to join the daily noon strategy meetings and soon I was asked to direct the emergency operation.

The way the emergency program came into being made a lasting impression on me and gave me a deep understanding and appreciation of the strength of the Christian church. At one of the first meetings I attended the issue was determining the best way to meet the needs of the victims—people whose homes had been burned, had been injured or were forced to evacuate their homes. Many people needed emergency housing, clothing, food, medical treatment and transportation. Others were willing to donate these resources. A problem of huge proportions was to get the resources moved to where the needs were.

Someone at the meeting voiced the opinion, "What we need is an agency or organization of some kind that has branches in the central city where the problems are and in the urban and suburban areas where most of the resources are—like a bank, for instance, but there are not near enough bank branch offices for the network we need." Everyone bemoaned the lack of a sorely needed network. If only there was such an agency of government or some such in the metro area that could be used for the collection and distribution of resources. We continued to ponder the problem of how we could manage the situation without such a network, when an unexpected suggestion changed the tone of the meeting. "What about the churches?" someone hesitantly asked. There was an electric silence as the light came on in the minds of the people seated around the conference table. The gathering came alive as one after another commented about the possibilities of using the Christian church for the emergency network we needed.

It was an amazing realization that we, especially the clergy, had overlooked the obvious. The dawning of this idea radically changed the way we saw the church's role in the crisis, and the group began to make specific plans and assignments to activate a network of suburban and neighborhood churches as centers to which volunteers could report, serve as possible emergency shelters or drop-off points for materials and foodstuffs. Since there were officials from all the major denominations at this meeting, they were in position to put the word out to their local congregations and get maximum coöperation.

So a very significant structure and system grew out of this suggestion. Several social-action buffs, including myself, attended those meetings. We were among the severest critics of the church for its poverty of social concern and involvement, yet now we saw, perhaps for the first time, that the church was the only institution in our society that could effectively deal with such a major social crisis.

We had discovered the gold in the church's earth and went about mining it with more pride in the church and more excitement about its place in the community than we had ever had. We had labored in the vineyard of social action with a self-image of organizational inadequacy, feeling like second-class social action citizens, just giving meager support to the public agents who were the bona fide tillers of the field. Suddenly we were the front runners. We had found our *cosa nostra,* our thing, our supremely valuable strength and facility for such a social crisis. Since that time, I have never again seen the church as a 90-pound social action weakling.

In one sense the Detroit experience opened my eyes to something that had been there all along but that I had never confronted before. In the years since Detroit I have seen the Christian church move into the breach all across our country time and again in a wide spectrum of crises and disasters and do what no other organization could do as quickly and effectively. I cannot imagine why I did not perceive this in the civil-rights movement of the '50s and '60s. It should have been evident to me that this movement would never have happened had it not been for the support from churches and religious communities throughout the country. From its most prominent leaders to a great percentage of the foot soldiers in the marches, its most forceful impetus came from the churches.

Blind as I had been to it, I came away from working in the Detroit Emergency Center much prouder of the unique value and comprehensiveness of the church's ministry. Now I realize that working in and on behalf of the Christian church is working in and for the chief agent for change and healing in our society. My eyes have been continually opened to see the myriad of ways the Christian church's ministry changes, influences and enhances peoples lives as no other organization ever could. Not only is the church equipped for dealing with the crises, natural and social, into which people are often thrown, but I am convinced this was one of the basic, if largely unseen, purposes for the creation of the church.

The characteristic response of church people to crises in the world is a foundational plank on which a renewing effort can be built. It is a natural place to start. We can find consolation as well as practical impetus in the realization that we are actually not faced with changing church people into social activists. Renewal of the church's social ministry does not require bringing something entirely new to its ministry; it requires leading our people from their natural sporadic response to human need and suffering to a more continual and comprehensive one.

"Dear Lord, please help us to appropriate the gifts you have given your church in a vital and continual ministry. Amen."

20

Let's Talk

Keep these words that I am commanding you today in your heart. Recite them to your children and talk about them when you are at home and when you are away, when you lie down and when you rise (Dt 6:6-7).

For scores of people the church, when at its best, has been a haven for those who could find no other place to get help or support for their problems. For countless people, the church, or a group in a local church, has provided a community of genuine caring when none could be found elsewhere.

It has always struck me as revealing a major shortcoming of the church that so many alcoholics and addicts cannot find recovery through its ministries, but when they become involved in an Alcoholics Anonymous, Narcotics Anonymous or any of the Twelve-Step groups, many of them experience a sustained recovery. This is not true in every case, of course, but for literally thousands of people it has been. What do these groups offer that is not found in our churches?

There are several differences. They meet more often, they have only one purpose, their anonymity encourages honest discussion about one's problems, they have a bond of like suffering, and because of these factors they get to know one another far more intimately than do most members of a local church. But the main

What's the Matter with the Church?

difference is what produces all of these other differences: at their meetings they all talk freely about their problems and their spiritual experience, or the lack of it.

In our church meetings, when there is any discussion at all, it is not very intimate or personal. The atmosphere is just not conducive for "letting it all hang out." In fact, it would seem inappropriate in those settings. This, I think, is extremely basic to the other problems the contemporary church has. There is something about frank and honest community dialogue that promotes healing.

The Twelve-Step programs foster healing and spiritual growth for these problems to a degree that our churches' ministries do not. Why is this important for the church?

First, we must remember the spiritual situation is actually the same for addicts and non-addicts. Christian faith sees all people as being in need of reconciliation with God, as being separated from God and in need of union with God. This is why so many people who are not alcoholics or addicts find so much support in Twelve-Step programs. The spiritual power needed to help addicts recover is the power that all of us need.

Substance and behavior addiction actually provides perhaps the clearest model for the nature of sin and redemption. This is not to deny the medical fact that addiction is a disease. It is both sin and disease. All disease is sin in the sense that it is separation from God. It is just not directly moral sin in most cases. And all human life apart from God has the essential character of addiction. In many instances we cannot change our various forms of self-centered behavior, and they are legion, without the help of a "Power greater than ourselves." The addicts who recover discover that the best, and in many cases the only, way to experience this Power is through honest discussion with other addicts.

This kind of communication also expands the knowledge of the spiritual life to a level that cannot be gained from sermons or through the traditional educational models that most churches use. There are scores of people in recovery groups who over the years of their participation have gained much knowledge and wisdom.

Many of them who have very little formal education converse about subjects on levels that rival others with graduate degrees. Given the quality of education in our churches, we should be envious of these recovery programs.

Open, frank and honest discussion also expands the sources of inspiration for its participants that is so critical for the degree of commitment needed for the effort to live by spiritual principles. Many times I have attended an AA meeting and sat there wishing I could see in our church meetings the level of inspiration that sustains so many alcoholics and addicts in their commitment to live by the principles of their recovery program.

Another product of this honest discussion that the church needs a great deal more of is overt, intimate affection. One of the main objectives of the Christian church has always been that its members would demonstrate great love for one another. "Now that you have purified your souls by your obedience to the truth so that you have genuine mutual love, love one another deeply from the heart" *(1 P 1:22)*.

Such love cannot be expressed among the members of our churches unless they engage in conversations where they get to know one another on personal levels. Opportunities for such discussions are too rarely available at our church gatherings. Anyone who visits an average AA meeting cannot help but notice the affection members of the fellowship have for one another and the lengths they are willing to go to help each other as well as those alcoholics still suffering from the illness.

No wonder John Wesley, founder of the Methodist movement, pleaded the case for "little societies" and "bands" with such urgent passion. He warned that if Methodists ever lost these small groups that had so enriched their lives and their movement, they would lose something vital and central to their ministry and mission. We can sadly attest to how right Wesley was for even Methodist churches lost "little societies" long ago.

Nothing *matters* more for the renewal of the church in our time than its need for a greater degree of a loving community.

This cannot take place unless its members come to know one another at personal levels through encounters of open and honest discussion. A religious institution can function quite well without it, but *koinonia*, the quality and style that is appropriate for the Body of Christ, absolutely depends upon it.

"Dear Lord, may we open our lives and minds and hearts to one another and may we have such mutual affection for one another that the Body of Christ will be an incomparable force of love and new life in the world. Amen."

21

Let's Have Fun

As for those who in the present age are rich, command them not to be haughty, or to set their hopes on the uncertainty of riches, but rather on God who richly provides us with everything for our enjoyment (1 Tm 6:17).

One of the most interesting *matters* in the history of the church's ministry is the role it has played at various times and places to provide people with entertainment. From its entrance into Europe through most of the 18th Century the church was responsible for the majority of the dramatic performances on the Continent and in Britain. It seemed the most natural thing for the church to promote entertainment for people. One of its primary ministries has always been to enrich the quality of human life, and the richness of social life would not have had much depth without some form of entertainment.

From the early American colonies to the turn of the 19th Century, the church was the main community center in countless small towns and rural communities in this country. It was the social center as well as the religious center. Given the needs of those times, this was a very natural way to serve the people of a parish.

There is a more basic reason why the church accepted the responsibility of providing entertainment. By it's very nature, the

Christian faith is not a private, individual *matter*. It is communal in character. As the doctrines of the church were becoming codified, one of the strongest affirmations was *novum salus ex ecclesiam* – no salvation outside the church. No one ever became a follower of Jesus Christ apart from the ministry of the church in some form. If salvation is in itself a communal phenomenon, an experience of Christian community, it would seem there could not be nearly as rich a sense of community if the members of a fellowship do not share some form of entertainment. It is evident to me that there is not near enough genuine enjoyment in our worship services.

A church member in Macon, Georgia once said to me, "I don't like it when you joke in church. We should be sad in church." I have always thought people in too many worship services behave like they believe that, but I had never heard it actually expressed.

The church's worship, stewardship and ministry are serious *matters*, but even solemnity does not exclude enjoyment. There are many somber experiences that have, of necessity, lighter sides. Seriousness itself is often the mother of humor and delight. As critical as their work is, doctors and nurses are known for their humor and exuberant social activities. No doubt it is the "letting off steam" phenomenon. I have never been to a funeral or a visitation at a funeral home that I didn't see small groups of people standing around remembering the good times. It might seem inappropriate, but it is natural because it pushes the sadness back and makes it more bearable.

There are no fellowships that deal with heavier topics than Alcoholics Anonymous groups, yet they are known for their efforts to supply a good time to all who attend. These people have a predisposition, a disease, that is fatal if it is not arrested. In any addict's life, there has been untold pain, for addicts as well as their families, friends and professional associates. But AA meetings usually are not somber and sedate. Their pleasure and humor do not merely come from "letting off steam," but also from a rich sense of gratitude at deliverance from an awful, progressive suffering and death—to a new freedom.

Enjoyment has an unparalleled attracting force. It is much easier to get people to come to a gathering that is pleasurable than to one that is uninteresting or dull. A powerful motivating force for people to become part of a church is the sense that our ultimate destiny is to be joyous and happy. By the same token, becoming a follower of Jesus Christ is a far more appealing venture when it is shown that, as C.S. Lewis said, "Joy is the serious business of heaven." The Good News is that our destination is not sorrow and death. Jesus' witness, as the Early Church presents it, is that beyond our earthly demise we will go to be with Christ in an everlasting joyous fulfillment. It is difficult to assess just how much this hope is responsible for motivating people to join the church, but we can safely say it is considerable.

Thus to be true to Christ's message there needs to be a strong element of enjoyment, in whatever form is appropriate for a given congregation at each church gathering. Instead of dreading to have to go to church knowing you will not enjoy it, we should be able to anticipate going to a worship service or activity as a most pleasurable experience.

Joy is a repeated theme throughout the Hebrew and Christian Scriptures. When Jesus prayed for the unity of his followers in his famous intercession in John 17, he included a request that his followers would experience the joy he experienced: "But now I am coming to you, and I speak these things in the world so that they may have my joy made complete in themselves" *(v. 13)*.

We cannot totally equate enjoyment and entertainment with what the Scriptures refer to as joy, but spiritual joy is consistent with genuine, wholesome humor and pleasurable experiences. It is definitely not consistent with an excessive sadness and seriousness. The renewal of the church must include the promotion of a genuine, spontaneous joyful atmosphere in our worship services and other congregational gatherings. It's obvious, isn't it, enjoyment in life really *matters*.

22

Let's Get Together

"We are living in an age that needs, and needs desperately, a growing worldwide Christian fellowship" (Kenneth Scott Latourette).

The unity of the followers of Christ is a major emphasis in the New Testament, and it could be argued that divisions in the Christian church are the most serious failings in its life and work. To refer again to John 17, most of Jesus' great prayer for his followers is devoted to this issue, but perhaps the most representative verse of the passage is: "I in them and you in me, that they may become completely one, so that the world may know that you have sent me and have loved them even as you have loved me" *(v. 23)*.

Paul sees this unity as no less than a function of how much Christian love we "put on" and cites it as being above all the Christian virtues. "Above all, clothe yourselves with love, which binds everything together in perfect harmony" *(Col 3:14)*, "making every effort to maintain the unity of the Spirit in the bond of peace" *(Ep 4:3)*. The aim of God's giving gifts of ministry to the followers of Christ is to equip the fellowship of believers "until all of us come to the unity of the faith and of the knowledge of the Son of God, to maturity, to the whole measure of the full stature of Christ" *(Ep 4:13)*.

Although always having had some witness in the church's life, the ecumenical movement as we know it today had fledgling beginnings in the 1930s and '40s, but did not begin to get real traction until the early '50s. It came into being largely among the clergy because of a growing awareness that the divisions in the church are the expressions of a blatant disobedience to our Lord. It is to the enduring credit of denominational leaders that the movement had its greatest impetus among them and many of the clergy who supported it.

But the denominational leaders and pastors were willing to go only so far and it is to their discredit that in recent years the uniting movement has become stymied at national and international levels. There are many things different communions and local churches do together, but the ecumenical movement as such has reached a point where it is apparently losing rather than gaining momentum. I have observed many instances of the ecumenical movement "running out of steam" in all the areas of the country in which I have served. It would seem to me that there are at least four reasons for this:

First, the denominational leaders and clergy lost interest in the effort as the reality of union came into sharper focus, and they began to see beyond the noble ideal to specific and practical details, some of which seemed to threaten their power bases.

Second, in an increasingly complicated world the interest in ecumenicity among them decreased because church leaders faced so many more responsibilities and difficulties along with severe budget cuts. Consequently they had less wherewithal to support efforts beyond their basic responsibilities.

Third, as they moved closer toward some form of union, they became more protective of their own and less willing to give up or sacrifice many of their organizational patterns.

Fourth, the various denominations cannot perceive ways to resolve their conflicting doctrinal positions. At the local level, most pastors and denominational leaders do not have serious difficulties with exploring ways to overcome or live with the doctrinal differences, but many face pressures against ecumenical efforts from their lay constituents who often are vocal and unrelenting in their opposition.

Since the movement was fueled from the beginning by denominational leaders and clergy, there never were many of the laity enthusiastically committed to ecumenicity. Thus the declining interest of denominational staff and pastors has been the decisive factor in the demise of the movement.

Of course, the denominational organizations are clearly the central forces in galvanizing the church's divisions, not so much in terms of individuals and their attitudes, but in terms of organizational structures. The denominations exist for the most part as separated and insulated institutions. The walls between them have been strongly built; attempts to bring them down or lower them are resisted and so few serious attempts to do so have been made. The denominations remain in place with forces of habit and tradition that will keep them in familiar patterns. I doubt these "strongholds" could be leveled or lowered by human efforts alone. Our "weapons" for this task, as is the case with most genuine renewal, must be essentially spiritual in nature. "For the weapons of our warfare are not merely human, but they have divine power to destroy strongholds" *(2 Co 10:4)*.

It seems clear that the progressive suicide of the denominations in their present forms is the only hope for the renewal of church unity. As the denominations move closer to their demise (as they are obviously doing) hopefully the churches and denominational staffs will become convinced that the situation must be changed. It is a sad commentary, but it appears that only their desire to survive in whatever form they can will motivate them to make the radical changes needed for the development of genuine church unity.

Internal conflicts are raging in the denominations in our time. Most are unaware of how serious the situation is. I had not actually thought about the situation in crisis proportions until a friend and fellow pastor pointed out to me that as the church entered the 21st Century every one of the major denominations was involved in serious internal conflicts that have continued unabated, and in many quarters are increasingly more hostile and tumultuous. In Southern Baptist ranks the issue is the "verbal inspiration" and "inerrancy" of the Scriptures. In most of the others the conflicts are about the ordination of women (This is also an issue among Southern Baptists, but the conflict does not extend to as many of its churches) or homosexuals. Where these conflicts will lead in the future is not yet clear, but it does not look promising because there are few signs or indications of significant reconciliation. One wonders if we are witnessing the fall of the "Kingdom of Saul". But the insurgence of the "Kingdom of David" is yet unseen.

It has always amazed me how denominational staff people are so protective of their traditions. Seldom do you find such protectiveness among lay people, but denominational staff seem to hold their traditions as uniquely sacred. Increasingly as time has passed since the original disputes and interpretations that formed the different denominations, lay people have shown little interest in or commitment to particular denominational doctrines or organizational models, except for remaining in the one they were brought up in. The advocacy for the denominations mainly comes from the clergy.

Having served in several denominations I have observed that there is not actually a great deal of difference among lay people as to what they believe, aside from the vocal minority to which we have referred. Now and then pastors will remind their parishioners what their distinctive beliefs are supposed to be, but they never seem to have much interest in the subject. So why can't we let them forget the reasons they are supposed to be separated from one another? It is apparent to me if we left this problem to the lay people, we could move toward unity a great deal faster and with less conflict.

This would seem to contradict what I have said about the pressures against ecumenism coming for the most part from the laity, but this pressure, while very vocal and persistent, does not come from the majority of church people. Most demonstrate little interest in the historic denominational distinctions. I have noticed many times a thinly veiled suspicion on the part of denominational staff people and some clergy of pastors who have served in another denomination. This so-called "loyalty" blatantly contradicts one of the main principles of Scripture, but they remain blind to this obvious inconsistency. "'You abandon the commandment of God and hold to human tradition.' Then he said to them, 'You have a fine way of rejecting the commandment of God in order to keep your tradition!'" (Mk 7:8-9).

What interpretations do they put on passages like these that allow them to think they do not apply to their denominational traditions? We frequently hear references to "our great tradition," or "our reformed tradition" as if they superseded Christ's commands. None of these people are that ignorant. This has been a case of classic denial. In a world that needs love in so many places for so many people, Christians are supposed to be living witnesses of an extraordinary love. In the Early Church the Christians seemed to have done that well. Tertulliam quoted third century "heathens" as commenting on their extraordinary love for one another. "Look," they say, "how they love one another" (for they themselves hate one another); "and how they are ready to die for each other" (for they themselves are readier to kill each other) (Apologeticum 39:7).

What seems to be most missing in the divided church is the love which is to bind us together "in perfect harmony." Instead we hear things like, "We love them but we can't be in the same church with them." Obviously, these kinds of remarks really express a lack of the love which binds everything together. It is *agape* love that accepts people with beliefs that are different from ours and genuinely shares a community of faith with them.

The world does not need an example of a "love" in which people cannot get along in shared communities and efforts. There is more than enough of that in the world without the church contributing to it. So the main cause of divisions in the church and a resistance to overcoming them is the lack of a basic Christian faith and a disobedience to the command that we are to put on this love which "binds everything together in perfect harmony." We simply do not have enough love. Would that there was more the attitude that John Wesley expressed, "If you love Christ, give me your hand."

The lack of love for one another among Christians has caused completely absurd divisions. The First Congregational Church I served in Connecticut is quite a large facility that is three blocks up the street from the Second Congregational Church, which is also quite a large facility. ! I was told the circumstances that divided the two congregations years ago was a disagreement over expanding the facilities. What they obviously lacked was the "love which binds everything together in perfect harmony." This is a situation that is duplicated in many places all over the country.

Obviously members of such battling churches do not spend much energy on preserving Christian unity or maintaining the unity of the Spirit in the bond of peace, which is why you hear everywhere among people outside the church, "They talk about love but they can't even get along with each other." What an example! What a powerful witness it would be if Christians around the world would realize that people who say this are right and reach out to one another in an effort to begin the hard work of putting the Body of Christ back together again.

There is an important practical issue here. There is a crying need to pool resources. There is probably no example anywhere of fragmentation and duplication comparable to the Christian church. What would it be like if we put them all together, human resources as well as material and financial, and organized them under one functional umbrella? It is difficult to imagine all that could be done if various communions somehow combined their efforts.

One of my most enjoyable fantasies is imagining all kinds of comprehensive, global, organizational and missional structures and efforts in a unified church. It is exciting to think about the incredible possibilities for what would be the largest and most influential single organization in human history taken to the fullest realization of its potential. I have commented on a number of ways in which the church has shown itself to be the greatest institution on earth. What would it be if we all really got together?

The numerical size of a unified Christian church is impossible to predict, since on the one hand if it were renewed to its true ministry and purpose, it would probably have a greatly reduced size. On the other, there is no telling how many more people might be won to serve the challenging and meaningful lordship of Jesus Christ if the church were to strengthen its fellowship and its message. Just offering the opportunity of faithfulness to the authentic Christian message would be an attractive invitation to the kind of people who make the best disciples.

We go in the wrong direction when we make the Gospel less challenging in order to attract more people. If we invited seekers to true discipleship, we would appeal to the many who want to be a part of something rather than members of an audience. One can be entertained seeing a play from the balcony, but it is immeasurably more meaningful and rewarding to be among the actors.

Making the decisive efforts that renewal would involve might offset the numerical losses the church would experience through the purification of its message and ministry. But even if there were fewer members, the smaller church would be infinitely more faithful to its Lord and therefore more effective in its mission. A unified Christian church may be only a delightful and unattainable ideal, but it is also a vision. Each step toward it is a step closer to what God wants from us.

And there is one approach to that vision that I believe has realistic possibilities. The term "umbrella" implies getting most of the communions to be under one organizational roof in some form, while remaining essentially what they are. This would leave each free to retain its particular doctrine, mission and identity, but it would involve a definite pooling of resources and move us along the path toward a truly unified church.

In whatever form and in whatever beginning, let us for the sake of our Lord make some serious efforts to move the church toward one Body of Christ.

23

He's the One

"To accomplish so great a work, Christ is always present in his church" (Second Vatican Council).

The renewal of the church would be such an easy task if the members of the Christian church were all perfected saints. However, the church is a communion of sinners, so the failings and shortcomings of the church are all expressions of the imperfections of its members. We cannot expect this will ever change completely. We can experience renewal, become more obedient to our Lord, grow more in grace, have more of the mind of Christ and we can be "pressing on to perfection" *(John Wesley)*, but we cannot eradicate the imperfections of the church because we cannot banish the sins of us as members. Much of the criticism that is logged against the church overlooks this immutable fact. The renewal of the church involves, not the perfection of its members, but a widespread willingness to be honest about their sinfulness, a continual and sincere attitude of repentance and a self-conscious commitment to be obedient to our Lord's instructions for the church.

Admittedly this is quite an order. However, it is a possibility for redeemed sinners, since it is, in the final analysis, not we who bring renewal whenever it comes; we believe it is our Lord who brings it. The church of Jesus Christ does not belong to us. Since it is Christ's church, it is imperative that we should not embark on making decisions and plans for any property or ministry without consulting the owner. We are only stewards of the Church, the greatest of Christ's gifts to his disciples, and stewards of a property are judged almost entirely by how well they carry out the owner's wishes.

If we are to launch such a comprehensive effort for renewal as I am proposing, it will almost certainly be a dismal failure if we are not careful in the beginning and all along the way to consult "the Head of the Church." It is a spiritual insult of the worst order when we seek to do something in Christ's church without first carefully seeking his counsel. Any effort for the renewal of the church is principally and primarily a corporate engagement in prayer. Before we touch anything about the church, we must approach the task with a balance of utmost commitment to very aggressive efforts on the one hand and reverent carefulness to ascertain the will of our Lord on the other.

But we do not have to become overly anxious about this. God will not require perfection of imperfect creatures in any venture. We dare not, however, overlook making continual efforts to seek Christ's guidance. This is not only important because of our sinfulness, but also because our finite minds are grossly insufficient for the task. To be effective in our efforts we need an overflowing measure of God's wisdom and power.

Only God, in Jesus Christ, is able to bring off such a huge and difficult task as a major renewal of his church. We must not attempt to get God to join our efforts; we must commit ourselves to joining God's plans. We must first seek to know the nature and methods for renewal that God's wisdom counsels.

Each one of the *matters* to which we have devoted a chapter in our discussion, taken alone, would be far greater than the resources at our disposal and greater than the number of people willing to work intentionally for the renewal of them. So obviously the whole realm of renewal would seem to be impossible if we were limited to human resources. We must determine from the Lord how to put together a strategic plan for those disciples who share a passion for renewal.

The first stage of renewal must be the recruitment of all those in every communion and congregation who share this passion and urge them to join in a concerted effort of prayer. The apostle Paul was quite confident that Christian conversion and growth in Christ, the process of transformation, is one of a renewed mind. "Be transformed by the renewing of your minds, so that you may discern what is the will of God – what is good and acceptable and perfect" (Rm 12:2).

When we face honestly the incontrovertible fact that real renewal depends entirely upon attitudinal change on the part of many clergy as well as many of the people in our pews, it becomes all the more evident that the task is impossible for human abilities and strengths. We can plan many things, but we cannot determine the responses people make to our plans.

Only God working in the minds and hearts of people can accomplish significant renewal, but when we realize that God surely wants the renewal of his church, we can confidently trust that the impossibility of the undertaking may be swept aside by an infusion of "Spirit".

What's the Matter with the Church?

24

Realizing the Vision

Where there is no vision, the people perish (Pr 29:18).

We are not talking about bringing the perfect church into being. We are talking about having before us a vision of what the perfect church would look like and taking steps that are possible, however short, to move our current church in that direction. If our efforts are organized and strategically planned there is no telling how much of the vision we can realize. (Wouldn't it be wonderful if God's church became God's movement again, to whatever degree? And wouldn't it be wonderful to be involved in a missional movement instead of an institutional one for a change?)

Our starting place is to call apart those who have the "salt" and the "fire," and those who will sincerely seek others with special gifts. This is first. How I wish my denomination would realize why our evangelism programs do not work very well. We cannot have evangelism without the power and passion that drives it. Reaching customers is not the first priority of a business. Having a good product is the first priority. We cannot give the salt and the fire to everyone in our churches; we cannot give it to most of them, but we can seek out the ones who are genuinely receptive to them and develop them into a renewal corps within the church.

We can call together all who are willing not only to change but who enthusiastically welcome it and who encourage frank discussion about "what's the *matter* with the church." We can call on these Christians to target those grotesque contradictions in our congregations between the Christian values we preach and the behavior of so many of our members and initiate self-conscious efforts to discourage them. As members of this renewal group, we can insist on some caring disciplinary measures for lay people as well as clergy who engage in behavior that violates Christian principles.

We can clearly and enthusiastically affirm our desire and conviction that our churches be open to any and all people. We can organize discussion groups that foster frank and honest conversations to encourage spiritual growth and deal with our problems. We can bring together ecumenical organizations in our communities and combine our resources to recruit Christian disciples and address the problems of crime, poverty, education and justice. We can intentionally identify and implement ways to make our congregational worship and life more enjoyable and interesting and even exciting. And we can call upon our churches to make Christian education genuinely more educational.

Let us not be so intimidated by the enormity of the task that we do nothing. Let us rather pick up our paltry amount of "rolls and fishes" and head into the great mass of hungry people with the faith born of experience that God will somehow expand our little store until it is more than sufficient. If we are able to move the church any distance at all toward the realization of the vision, we will be the better for it and, more importantly, the church will be the better for it.

I hope you are as tired as I am of cursing the darkness. Many of our candles are quite small, but if we light them and put them all together, the glory of the church will shine brighter in the world than it has ever shown before. Let us begin.

"Our Father, we do not ask that you follow our views in renewing your church. We ask rather that you inform us of your wisdom wherever our understanding fails. We earnestly pray that you use us wherever we can be your instruments, or that you use others, or that you work directly in your church to renew it. However you will, Lord, please bring renewal. We rejoice in the hope that your wisdom and power and love will bring your church to its finest life and work. Amen."

Additional copies of this book may be obtained
from your bookstore
or by contacting
Hope Publishing House
P.O. Box 60008
Pasadena, CA 91116 - U.S.A.
(626) 792-6123 / (800) 326-2671
Fax (626) 792-2121
E-mail: hopepub@sbcglobal.net
www.hope-pub.com